Church History

Church History

Faith Handed On

Catholic Basics
A Pastoral Ministry Series

Kevin L. Hughes, Ph.D.

Thomas P. Walters, Ph.D.
Series Editor

NATIONAL CONFERENCE FOR
CATECHETAL LEADERSHIP

LOYOLAPRESS.
3441 N. ASHLAND AVENUE
CHICAGO, ILLINOIS 60657

NIHIL OBSTAT: Rev. Daniel J. Mahan, S.T.B., S.T.L.
Censor Librorum

IMPRIMATUR: Rev. Msgr. Joseph F. Schaedel
Vicar General/Moderator of the Curia

Given at Indianapolis, Indiana, on February 19, 2001

The *nihil obstat* and *imprimatur* are official declarations that a book is free of doctrinal and moral error. No implication is contained herein that those who have granted the *nihil obstat* and *imprimatur* agree with the content, opinions, or statements expressed.

Cover Design: Other Brother Design
Cover Illustration: Steve Snodgrass
Interior Illustrations: Other Brother Design

Library of Congress Cataloging-in-Publication Data

Hughes, Kevin L.
    Church history : faith handed on / Kevin L. Hughes.
    p. cm. – (Catholic basics)
    Includes bibliographical references.
    ISBN 0-8294-1723-0
    1. Catholic Church–History. 2. Church history. I. Stasiak, Kurt, 1952–
Means of grace, ways of life. II. Title. III. Series.

BX945.3 .H84 2001
270–dc21   2001029644
                                                     CIP

ISBN: 0-8294-1723-0

Published by Loyola Press, 3441 N. Ashland Avenue, Chicago, Illinois 60657 U.S.A.
© 2002 The National Conference for Catechetical Leadership.
All rights reserved. No part of this book may be reproduced, stored in a retrieval system, or transmitted in any form or by any means, electronic, mechanical, photocopying, recording, or otherwise, without the prior permission of the publisher.
Manufactured in the United States of America.

05   Bang   5   4   3

Table of Contents

About The Series   vii

Certification Standards: National Resouces for
    Church Ministry   viii

Introduction: Why Church History?   x

Chapter 1: Faith in Formation   1

Paul's Dilemma: Christians and Jews in the First Century   2

Insiders and Outsiders: Was the Early Church "Catholic"?   4

Rome Against Christians: The Story of Perpetua   12

Drawing the Threads Together:
    The Birth of the Catholic Church   18

For Reflection   19

Chapter 2: Faith Established   20

Toleration and Its Discontents   21

The Search for Purity in a "Lukewarm" Church   24

Establishment and Collapse: 364–476 A.D.   30

The Church at the End of the Empire   36

For Reflection   38

Chapter 3: The Faith of Christendom   39

The Birth of the Medieval World (500–700):
    Gregory of Tours and Gregory the Great   40

The "Carolingian Renaissance" and the Ideal of
    Christendom (800–1000)   47

The Gregorian Reform (1050–1120): The Pope as
    Abbot to the World   49

The High Middle Ages (1100–1300): The Flowering of
    Religious Life and the Birth of Scholasticism   55

For Reflection   58

CHAPTER 4: **Faith Divided**   59

Papal Authority in Crisis: The Avignon Popes and
    the Great Papal Schism   60

Restoration or Reform? Papal Indulgence and Lay Piety   63

The Varieties of Reform   73

For Reflection   79

CHAPTER 5: **Faith in a New World**   80

St. Ignatius and the Jesuit "Way of Proceeding"   81

The World at War: Europe in the Seventeenth Century   90

From Momentum to Inertia: The Catholic Church on the
    Eve of Revolution   92

For Reflection   94

CHAPTER 6: **Faith in an Age of Revolutions**   95

The Church and the Scientific Revolution   96

Shots Heard 'Round the World: Revolution in America and
    France   97

Pius IX: Reform and Reaction   102

America and Americanism   105

The Early Twentieth Century: Catholic Modernism and
    the Stirrings of Change   108

American Catholicism at Mid-Century   109

For Reflection   111

CHAPTER 7: **Conclusion: Faith Handed on to
the Third Millennium**   112

Bibliography   121

Acknowledgments   123

About the Author   124

About the Series

Catholic Basics: A Pastoral Ministry Series offers an in-depth yet accessible understanding of the fundamentals of the Catholic faith for adults, both those preparing for lay ministry and those interested in the topics for their own personal growth. The series helps readers explore the Catholic tradition and apply what they have learned to their lives and ministry situations. Each title offers a reliable introduction to a specific topic and provides a foundational understanding of the concepts.

Each book in the series presents a Catholic understanding of its topic as found in Scripture and the teachings of the Church. Each of the authors has paid special attention to the documents of the Second Vatican Council and the *Catechism of the Catholic Church*, so that further learning can be guided by these core resources.

Chapters conclude with study questions that may be used for small group review or for individual reflection. Additionally, suggestions for further reading offer dependable guides for extra study.

The initiative of the National Conference of Catechetical Leadership led to the development of an earlier version of this series. The indispensable contribution of the series editor, Dr. Thomas Walters, helped ensure that the concepts and ideas presented here are easily accessible to a wide audience.

Certification Standards: National Resources for Church Ministry

E ach book in this theology series relates to standards for theological competency identified in the resources listed below. Three national church ministry organizations provide standards for certification programs that serve their respective ministries. The standards were developed in collaboration with the United States Catholic Conference Commission on Certification and Accreditation. The fourth resource is the latest document, and it was developed to identify common goals of the three sets of standards.

Competency Based Certification Standards for Pastoral Ministers, Pastoral Associates and Parish Life Coordinators. Chicago: National Association for Lay Ministry, Inc. (NALM), 1994.

These standards address three roles found in pastoral ministry settings in the United States. The standards were the earliest to receive approval from the United States Catholic Conference Commission on Certification and Accreditation. Copies of the standards are available from the National Association for Lay Ministry, 5420 S. Cornell, Chicago, IL 60615-5604.

National Certification Standards for Professional Parish Directors of Religious Education. Washington, DC: National Conference for Catechetical Leadership, 1998.

NCCL developed standards to foster appropriate initial education and formation, as well as continuing personal and professional development, of those who serve as Directors of Religious Education (DREs). The standards address various areas of knowledge and abilities needed in the personal, theological, and professional aspects of the ministry. Also included is a code of ethics for professional catechetical leaders. Available from the National Conference of Catechetical Leadership, 3021 Fourth Street NE, Washington, DC 20017-1102.

NFCYM Competency-Based Standards for the Coordinator of Youth Ministry. Washington, DC: National Federation for Catholic Youth Ministry, 1996.

This document lays out the wide range of knowledge and skills that support ministry with young people as well as the successful leadership and organization of youth ministry wherever it may be situated. The standards are available from the National Federation for Catholic Youth Ministry, 415 Michigan Avenue NE, Suite 40, Washington, DC 20017-1518.

Merkt, Joseph T., ed. *Common Formation Goals for Ministry.* A joint publication of NALM, NFCYM, and NCCL, 2000.

Rev. Joseph Merkt compared the documentation of standards cited by three national organizations serving pastoral, youth, and catechetical ministries. The resulting statement of common goals identifies common ground for those who prepare persons for ministry, as well as for the many who wear multiple hats. Copies are available from NALM, NCCL, or NFCYM.

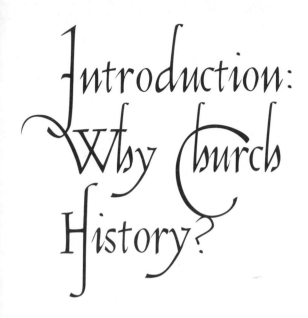

Introduction: Why Church History?

"Church history" is a clear conversation stopper. Whatever my answer when I'm asked what I do: "I'm a historian of Christianity" or "a Church historian" or "a historical theologian," I get the same blank gaze, the vague affirmation of "Oh, how interesting . . ." and the awkward search for another topic of conversation. I used to take this personally, but I don't anymore. I've come to realize that, for many people, each of those identifiers contains a word that awakens memories of fear or boredom or both—*history*.

"History" for many evokes a picture of a frumpy-looking teacher or professor droning on in monotone about people and events long passed. For some, it recalls late nights cramming names and dates before a chapter test or final exam. It may conjure up images of the most obscure and least useful branch of knowledge in the humanities. So-called "great deeds of dead white men," etc. Whatever the association, it is often not good. So what could be so interesting or important to directors of religious education about Church history?

What if we were to reframe this a bit? Try to put away all your preconceptions of what "history" is and try a new way of thinking about it. When I think about who I am as a person, I cannot help but think about where I come from. I want to know about my family history, my ethnic heritage, how my parents met— all those little details help me come to understand how I got to be the way I am. And it is a thrill to learn! How many of us have been plied with questions from our children: "How did you and Mom meet?" or "Tell me about when I was born." And how many of us have sat in awe and fascination when our parents or grandparents have told stories about "the old country" or the "good old days"? In a way, Church history is the same set of questions, the same stories, on a larger scale. It is the story of faith handed on, of how fallible human people, given by God to be members of the Body of Christ in the Church, have struggled to live out the Gospel in the very concrete circumstances of their lives for nearly two thousand years. If we stand within the Church, if we are the Church, then it is our story. And when we learn the story of our struggles, triumphs, and failures, we come to know more about who and what we are as a community of faith.

Whatever insights we receive we must in turn hand on to those who will follow us. The Good News received from the Apostles "is perpetuated in the Church by means of the Church herself. The entire Church, pastors and faithful, is responsible for its conservation and transmission" (*General Dirctory for Catechesis*, #43). We are responsible for the conservation and transmission of the truths of the Gospel. In large part, this can come from a prayerful study of Scripture and the teachings of the Church. But it can also come from the study of how others have conserved the Gospel and transmitted it to us. As we strive to embody the Body of Christ here, in North America, now, at the dawn of a new millennium, we can only benefit from the insight and wisdom—and even from the mistakes and missteps—of those who have striven to do the same in their own place and their own time. So what I will try to do in the few pages that follow is to give some broad sketches of how this has been done throughout the history of the Roman Catholic Church. I hope this work will serve more as an invitation than as a definitive word on the subjects treated here—an invitation to reflect and to explore the depths and riches of a tradition that flows so abundantly through two thousand years of Church history. For I am convinced that some knowledge of those depths and riches of the past will nourish your ministry in the Church of today.

Coming to Terms with the Topic: What Is Church History?

I like to think that the patron saint of Church historians is Luke, the Gospel writer. Luke begins his Gospel with the acknowledgment that "many have undertaken to set down an orderly account of the events that have been fulfilled among us," (1:1) but he wants to do a little bit more. Rather than just putting together some story or another that he has heard, Luke promises to do his homework first: *"I too decided, after investigating everything carefully from the very first, to write an orderly account . . ."* (1:3; emphasis added). Luke's Gospel and Acts of the Apostles are modeled upon traditional Greek histories of great people. Luke's effort represents the self-conscious work of a historian: gathering evidence, evaluating it for accuracy, and interpreting and recording it in an orderly fashion. But it is not only that, since Luke says he writes these things "for you, most excellent Theophilus, so that you may know the truth concerning the things about which you have been instructed" (Luke 1:3–4). Church history is always a narrative or story written for the Church, for those who are called "friend of God" (*theophilos* in Greek) to build up their faith.

This self-conscious intention sets Church history apart from generic "history," even if it is a "history of Christianity." Many historians claim to take a "value-neutral" stance toward the past, but the past matters deeply to the Church, and so it matters to the Church historian. This distinction does not mean, however, that Church history is necessarily propagandist, although that temptation certainly must be faced by anyone who tells the story of the Church. On the contrary, someone who tells that story for the Church needs to be aware both of her own "blind spots" or potential biases and of her responsibilities to the community in which she stands, to "get it right," to tell the truth of the Christian past in love and to the best of her ability. If from time to time this includes discussion of dark moments in which members of the Church failed to live up to the demands of Christian charity, then so be it. We can learn from past mistakes as well as past successes.

So what sort of story does the Church historian tell? I began by saying that it is the story of "faith handed on." In other words, Church history tells the story of the tradition of the Church (traditio is Latin for "handing over"). In his book *Tradition and Traditions*, the great Dominican theologian Yves Congar described tradition in three senses: First, tradition is the "transmission of the whole Gospel" in the Scriptures and the preached word, in the creeds and confessions of faith, in the sacraments and liturgical life, and in the moral life of the Church. This is the sense of tradition that we receive from Paul's First Letter to the Corinthians: "For I handed on to you as of first importance what I in turn had received: that Christ died for our sins in accordance with the scriptures, and that he was buried, and that he was raised on the third day in accordance with the scriptures" (1 Corinthians 15:3–4). It is in this sense that the *General Directory for Catechesis (GDC)* says, "The Gospel is conserved whole and entire in the Church: the disciples of Jesus Christ contemplate it and meditate upon it unceasingly; they live it out in their everyday lives; they proclaim it in their missionary activity" (#43). It is the message of redemption as it is proclaimed, believed, and lived.

Second, tradition is the self-conscious interpretation of the Gospel—above all, interpretation of the Scriptures—in the formation and teaching of the faithful. From the Apostles on, the Church receives the divine revelation of the Gospel not only as a lived reality, but also as the "deposit of faith," as a body of knowledge concerning the reality of God, humanity, and all creation to be received and interpreted by the intellect. In the Roman Catholic Church, faith in the Holy Spirit's presence entails faith in the Church's teaching office, the *magisterium*, to guide and protect this interpretation. Tradition in this sense is what Aidan Nichols, O.P., calls "the educative *milieu* [or context] for faith." It is the context in which we learn the truths of our faith.

Finally, says Congar, the term "tradition" can refer to particular moments, or what he calls "monuments of faith." These are elements within the history of the Church that seem to bear witness to and declare the Gospel itself in a distinctive and enduring way. Congar counts among these "monuments" the fathers and doctors of the Church, the papal encyclicals and pastoral letters of the Church, the witness of theologians, and even Christian art. Congar also includes as his last category of "monuments" what he calls "ordinary expressions of the Christian life." In this last category are included the lives of the saints, who have been called to "live [the Gospel] in a special manner."

A so-called "thick description" of Church history, then, would include all of these things, from Scripture and the dogmas of the faith, to the lives of the saints, to the way you and I and those who have gone before us bring the Gospel to life in our daily decisions. It would take a lifetime of scholarship to even begin to understand all these dimensions of our past as a Church. But we can benefit from even a taste of that rich past, and we can hand on what we have learned to others. That is the only goal and purpose of this little book: to offer a taste, and to invite us all to share it.

❧✝❧

FOR REFLECTION

1. What stories about your family, your community, or your roots have been important to you in your life? What makes these stories influential?

2. Are there particular "monuments" in the tradition—whether they are particular books or saints—that have influenced your life of faith? How have they influenced you?

3. Is there any relationship between a church's history and its ministry?

CHAPTER 1

Faith in Formation

I f the Christian Church can be traced back to the community that gathered around Jesus of Nazareth, then the Church faced its first crisis when their leader was arrested and executed. Faith in the Resurrection enabled the Apostles to overcome this challenge—indeed to see that death and the Resurrection that followed as the key to understanding who Jesus really was. In fact, as I mentioned in the Introduction, the Gospel of Luke and Acts, taken together, can be seen as a story showing that very sense of continuity through the crisis of the Crucifixion. Acts picks up the story where Luke leaves off, to show the Apostles, empowered by the Spirit, about the business of spreading the Gospel. Acts of the Apostles (along with the letters of Paul) bears witness to the earliest Church's attempt to answer the question, What does it take to be a disciple of Jesus? In a sense, all of Church history can be seen as an attempt to answer this question in particular times and places. But at this particular time, in the first century A.D., throughout the Roman Empire, the first and fundamental answers to the question were offered by that first apostolic generation of believers. In these earliest years, these answers came to Christians only through their struggles with both outsiders and insiders to stay faithful to the Gospel.

Paul's Dilemma: Christians and Jews in the First Century

Everyone knows the story of Saul, the Pharisee, the persecutor of the Christians, who was knocked off his horse on the road to Damascus and encountered the risen Christ. Saul, the zealous persecutor, became Paul, the zealous preacher. The Pharisee became an Apostle. His conversion gave him insight into the radical newness of the Gospel as a message open to Jews and Gentiles alike. Paul was convinced that Gentiles did not need to become Jews to accept the Gospel of Christ, but some of his fellow Apostles disagreed. His

Letter to the Galatians bears witness to the conflict over this very thorny issue, and in it, Paul gives his famous proclamation: "There is no longer Jew or Greek, there is no longer slave or free, there is no longer male and female; for all of you are one in Christ Jesus" (3:28). To some of the more conservative Apostles, especially James in Jerusalem, this radical statement seemed to cut away all that was good and right in the Jewish tradition. Paul seemed to want to abandon Judaism altogether.

But, even for Paul, it was not so easy to cut the ties to the Jewish faith. His Letter to the Romans represents his struggle to make sense of the relationship between the radical newness of the Gospel of Christ and the old covenant that God had made with Israel. If the Christ is the fulfillment of the old covenant, why did most Jews not convert? Could God have abandoned Israel in favor of the Gentiles? Paul's answer is clear: "I ask, then, has God rejected his people? By no means!" (Romans 11:1). But despite the clarity of his answer, the exact relationship between Jew and Gentile, between old covenant and new, remained unclear. Paul's dilemma remained unresolved even after his death (and, some would argue, it remains unresolved today).

What I have called "Paul's dilemma" is one of the first—and most bitter—struggles that the Christian Church faced in the earliest years of its life. In the year 62 A.D., James, the "brother of the Lord," was executed in Jerusalem by the Jewish high priest, with the support of a public mob. James had been the greatest advocate of retaining Jewish traditions among the Christians, and yet the high priest apparently considered him an enemy. With his death, those in favor of retaining ties to their Jewish past lost their center of influence, and they disappear from the historical record after about the year 66. Almost by default, it seems, the Gentile communities emerged as the successors to the Apostles. Any hope of reconciliation between Judaism and the new Christian communities was rapidly slipping away. The divisions between Christian and Jew became more and more pronounced, so that by the end of the first century, the final break was evident.

In the year 70, Jerusalem was sacked by the Romans to quell a Jewish rebellion. With their temple and capital destroyed, Jewish leaders quickly reorganized around the school at Jamnia, another city in Palestine, which then became the center of Jewish teaching. The assembled leaders at Jamnia declared that the canon of the Scriptures was closed and Jews should not look for any further revelation (including, it seems to be implied, a revelation from Jesus of Nazareth). In addition, by about the year 90, a sentence was added to the traditional *Eighteen Benedictions* that cursed "Nazarenes and heretics." The feeling was mutual: From the Christian side of the conflict, Ignatius, bishop of Antioch and martyr (d. 107–108) declared that "to profess Jesus Christ while following Jewish customs" was "an absurdity." The customs of Judaism were to Ignatius the "old, good-for-nothing leaven, now grown stale and sour" (Ignatius, *Letter to the Magnesians*, #10). The knot that bound Christians and Jews had been severed.

Insiders and Outsiders: Was the Early Church "Catholic"?

With all ties to the Jewish community cut, the earliest Christian communities were a bit at a loss to figure out what was a legitimate expression of Christian faith and what was out of bounds. The many communities spread throughout the Mediterranean world had been established by various missionary efforts, of which Paul's was only one. This meant that, at this earliest stage, there was no centralized authority or empire-wide structure, so the expressions of the Christian faith were potentially as many as there were individual churches. Some scholars have concluded that it is therefore best to speak of earliest "Christianities" rather than suggesting prematurely some unified notion of the Christian faith. It is certainly true that the Catholic Church as we know it today, with its well-structured universal hierarchy and authority centralized in Rome, did not take shape in the first few centuries. In the middle of the second century, we can begin to see evidence of bishops and priests (or presbyters, as some scholars prefer), and communication between these bishops established some common ground. But this earliest structure is a far cry from the hierarchical order that we now see in the Catholic and Orthodox churches. Rather, the story of early Christianity is the story of an emerging catholicity (with a small c), an emerging broad consensus on matters of faith and order, out of a wide variety of churches.

This is not to say that the Catholic and Orthodox churches' claims to be the "churches of the Apostles" are false, nor is it to claim that what emerged as the "orthodox faith" was an artificial invention. Rather, what I am suggesting is that the faith of the Apostles, the faith of Paul that he handed on as he had first received it, became more and more clarified as Christians confronted the challenges—both internal and external—that arose in those early years. Thus, when I speak in this chapter of an emerging "catholic Church" with a small *c*, I am not questioning or undermining the claims of the Roman Catholic Church and the Orthodox Church to have descended from the Apostles; rather, I am suggesting that we can see the lines of apostolic succession only in retrospect. This is akin to saying that each of us can rarely know whether what we are now doing is God's will or not, but we can often see the hand of Providence if we look back. So, too, the early Christians simply struggled to be faithful to Christ and, looking back, we can see the unbroken thread of faith woven through all their struggles.

MARCION: THE STRUGGLE OVER THE CANON OF SCRIPTURE

In about 140 A.D., a young man raised on the coast of the Black Sea arrived in Rome. He was the son of a bishop and a successful businessman in his own right. He was well-received by the church in Rome, due in part, perhaps, to the substantial donation he offered. But within a few years, the man, named

Marcion, began to proclaim a message that made the Roman church uneasy, to say the least. According to Marcion, Jesus had rejected the God of the Jews and proclaimed faith in a different God altogether that no one had known before. To prove his point, Marcion composed a work called the Antitheses that listed apparent contradictions between the Old Testament and Christian beliefs. He made another list, or canon, of the Christian writings that, in his opinion, taught this truth. On this list were only the letters of Paul and an edited version of the Gospel of Luke from which all the references to "Israel" had been omitted. Marcion represented the radical extreme of the reaction we have already seen in Ignatius of Antioch: the Jewish covenant is over, and it has been replaced by the Gospel. But this view was considered too extreme for the Roman community, and they excommunicated Marcion and returned his donation in 144.

Undeterred, Marcion traveled the Mediterranean until his death (ca. 160), setting up churches that survived for as much as two hundred years. But Marcion's message was determined to be out of bounds by the great majority of Christians: Christ had come to fulfill the Law, not to abolish it, and so faith in Christ meant faith in the God proclaimed in the Old Testament, the Creator, the God of Israel. In response to Marcion, Christians began to devise their own list of authoritative books, their own canon of Scripture, which included the books of the Jewish Scriptures as well as the newer Christian writings. Though the ties between Christians and Jews were severed, the earliest Christians affirmed that both parties believed in the one true God.

This consensus emerged only under the pressure that Marcion's teaching placed on the communities throughout the Mediterranean world. It is one of the cruel facts of history that firm conviction in the truth of a teaching emerges only from conflict. Under pressure from Marcion and others who seemed to go too far, a tentative unity began to emerge from the broad diversity of the first century and a half of Christianity. This tentative unity is what some scholars have called the Great Church or what we might begin to call the (small c) catholic Church.

MONTANISM: THE QUESTION OF AUTHORITY

The emerging catholic consensus faced another challenge from the followers of a trio of charismatic figures named Montanus, Priscilla, and Maximilla. The movement called itself the New Prophecy, but its opponents named it Montanism, after the male leader. Montanism began in Asia Minor in the mid-second century, when "the Three"—Montanus, Priscilla, and Maximilla—began preaching with enthusiasm about the Spirit's ongoing presence in the Church. The movement soon spread to North Africa and Rome. The Three proclaimed their message ecstatically (as if possessed by the Holy Spirit) and claimed to speak in the person of the Paraclete promised in John's Gospel. They exhorted their followers to observe rigorous practices of fasting and asceticism. They believed that the apocalyptic end was imminent and that the Heavenly Jerusalem would descend upon the city of Pepuza in Asia Minor. Despite some claims to the contrary, Montanists did not seem to differ with the emerging catholic Church's consensus on matters of doctrine and theology. Nonetheless, they were excommunicated in Rome in 177, probably for their undisciplined enthusiasm and perceived lack of respect for Church order and authority. In spite of this, in the early third century, Montanism gained its most famous member in Tertullian, an early apologist and theologian in North Africa, who, it seems, was persuaded by their passionate rigor.

Montanism presented the catholic Church with an interesting test case. Though the Montanists' doctrine was apparently sound, their loose, charismatic notion of authority was troubling. Could one rely upon the authority of one "caught up in the Spirit" to lead one faithfully in Christian life? Did the Spirit continue to speak to believers with special revelations, or was revelation now mediated through the ministry of word and sacrament by the successors to the Apostles, the bishops? If the conflict with Marcion had called the catholic Church to reaffirm its connection with the revelation of the Old Testament, the conflict with the Montanists "reinforced its conviction that revelation had come to an end with the apostolic age," as Henry Chadwick has said.

GNOSTICISM: THE QUESTION OF TRUE DOCTRINE

A final major factor in the emergence of the catholic consensus was the question of assimilation. No one could deny that Christians were immersed in the Hellenistic culture of the Roman Empire—the cultural context of the Greek paganism of the time. The task, then, was to articulate their faith in Christ in that language and context. Indeed, Hellenistic philosophy and culture offered tremendous resources for Christians to express and explore their faith in their particular lives of faith. But to what extent could Hellenistic culture be integrated with Christian faith? What in Hellenistic philosophy and religion was compatible with discipleship in Christ, and what should be rejected? Like so many other questions we have raised in this chapter, these are perennial questions for Christians in every culture. But as the catholic Church was in its infancy, these questions were brought especially to the fore by the phenomenon of Christian Gnosticism.

The terms *gnosticism* or *gnostic* come from the Greek word *gnosis*, which means "knowledge." Gnosticism thus refers to a set of beliefs in a saving knowledge.

This knowledge was not academic or rational knowledge. Rather, it referred to knowledge of divine secrets about the nature and destiny of human beings. It offered answers to the questions, Where do we come from? and Where are we ultimately going? Gnostics believed that this knowledge alone was enough to set them free from the illusions and darkness of the present world.

Gnosticism was never necessarily a coherent sect or church; rather, the term refers to similarities found across a number of different thinkers and texts in the second century, similar in many ways to the "New Age" phenomenon of the late twentieth century. Like New Age mythologies, Gnosticism seems to synthesize elements of many religious and philosophical traditions in the Hellenistic world: sectarian Jewish, Zoroastrian, and Platonic strands show up here and there. Scholars have disputed whether Gnostic mythologies pre-date Christianity or not, and it is difficult to say who is right. But the classic teachers of Gnosticism that we know of— Valentinus, Basilides, Ptolemy—believed that they had arrived at a true interpretation and a deeper understanding of the mission of Jesus through the lens of this "saving knowledge" of the cosmos and human destiny.

Gnostic myths share a general worldview, although the details of the picture may differ from teacher to teacher. For the Gnostic, the world as we know it is a dark place of evil, dominated by an evil god. This dark domain came to be when part of the brilliant fullness of the heavens (the *pleroma*, Greek for "fullness") fell from grace and was cast out. Human beings, or, more accurately, some "elect" human beings, have a soul that is a "spark of light" captured from the heavenly *pleroma* and trapped in the body. This spark is the true self of the elect, mired and imprisoned though it be in the physical body. Escape from this enslavement in the world of darkness can occur only if a heavenly revealer should come from the *pleroma* to grant the secret knowledge to a select few. With this knowledge, the divine spark can be released and return to the heavenly fullness that is its rightful home.

One can see that these myths share the rough outlines of traditional Jewish and Christian models of the angelic Fall and the Redemption offered by a divine figure, and one can readily imagine how easily the message of Jesus could be fit into this schema. Like Marcion, many Gnostics rejected the God of the Old Testament as the fallen creator of the world of darkness. Jesus then offers liberation from this fallen god with a path to return to "the Father" in the *pleroma*. (See *Catechism of the Catholic Church [CCC]*, #285 for some further explanation of Gnosticism.) But unlike Marcion, Gnostics believed that it was absurd to claim that Jesus, the heavenly revealer, actually died on the cross. Instead, Jesus only appeared to take on the form of a human being to deliver his message. (This denial that the Son took on flesh is called *docetism*, from the Greek *dokein*, "to appear." See *CCC*, #465.) Some Gnostic writings even tell of Jesus laughing from a distance as the dark powers look upon the cross at the dead body that he had used as a vessel and think they have killed him. Salvation comes not from the Incarnation, the life, the death, and the Resurrection of Jesus, but from the secret teachings he imparted to his followers.

Gnostic Christians possessed their own scriptures (the Gospel of Thomas is perhaps the most famous) and offered spiritual interpretations of the letters of Paul to demonstrate the truth of their claims. Indeed, in the twentieth century, some prominent scholars have suggested that Gnostic Christians have been unfairly judged and perhaps offered a more palatable alternative to what became the orthodox faith. However, in the judgment of non-Gnostic Christians, Gnostic teaching stepped beyond the limits of right faith in Jesus. Non-Gnostic Christians responded to Gnostic claims by emphasizing precisely those points that Gnostics called into question: Jesus' "Father" was none other than the Creator of the world. As they did against Marcion, Christians insisted upon the validity of the Old Testament as prophetic of the coming of Christ. They insisted upon the true Incarnation of Jesus and asserted that his suffering, death, and Resurrection in the flesh, far from being an illusion, was essential to Christian faith. For non-Gnostic Christians, it was clear that we are saved by the "Blood of the Lamb," not by some cosmic secret.

But to support these claims, non-Gnostic Christians had to arrive at criteria for evaluation; proof-texting from Paul or other Christian writings was a method that could be used by the Gnostics as well as the non-Gnostics. So how could one evaluate the authority and validity of what a Gnostic claimed was Christian?

Irenaeus of Lyons, whom some have called the "first systematic theologian," arrived at a solution: the *apostolic faith*. This apostolic faith was composed of two interrelated principles: Holy Scripture and the "rule of faith." According to Irenaeus, the Apostles had deposited the contents of Scripture and the rule of faith in the Church. Scripture for him included the Greek translation of the Old Testament (called the *Septuagint*) and a list of writings that he (for the first time) called the *New Testament* or *new covenant.* These writings were those that Irenaeus and other catholic thinkers could say with confidence were *apostolic*, meaning that they had some sort of close connection to the Apostles. For example, the Gospels of Matthew and John were believed to have been authored directly by the Apostles for which they are named, while Luke and Mark were considered to have been written under the direct authority of Paul and Peter, respectively. Irenaeus's New Testament looked much like our own, including the four Gospels (Matthew, Mark, Luke, and John), a collection of Paul's letters, Acts, Revelation, First Peter, and First and Second John. Apparently, the only difference between Irenaeus's canon and the Roman Catholic canon was his omission of James, Jude, Second Peter, and Hebrews. (*CCC*, #120 gives the Roman Catholic canon.)

This canon of Scriptures, both Old and New Testament, always has to be understood along with the other component of the apostolic faith, the "rule of faith." For Irenaeus, the rule of faith was a brief summary of the Christian belief in God's action in the world from creation to redemption in Christ and sanctification in the Spirit. Irenaeus never gave a set formula for the rule, but it functioned almost like a creed. The Church, he said, believes "in one God, the Father Almighty, Maker of heaven, and earth, and the sea, and all the things that are in them; and in one Christ Jesus, the Son of God, who became incarnate for our salvation; and in the Holy Spirit" (Irenaeus, *Adversus Haereses* 1.10.1). This basic statement of faith was drawn from Scripture, but it was also a necessary key to interpreting Scripture. In a famous image, Irenaeus compares Scripture to a mosaic, where each passage or book is one piece of the many that make the larger picture. The rule of faith is the plan or the blueprint that enables one to put the passages in the right order.

The dialectic, or back-and-forth, relationship between these two elements of the apostolic faith provided the emergent catholic Church with a sort of "checks and balances" set of criteria by which to evaluate an individual Christian's teaching and practices. For Irenaeus, these criteria were entrusted by the

Apostles to their successors, the bishops, or "overseers." With the guidance of this double deposit, the bishops were free to do more than react negatively to the teaching of people like Marcion or the Gnostics. They could lead the faithful into the process of providing positive norms for the life of Christian discipleship.

Rome Against Christians: The Story of Perpetua

Along with these internal struggles for definition of canon, authority, and doctrine, the early Christians also had to establish the Church's proper relationship to the external powers that be of those early centuries, the Roman Empire. Jesus of Nazareth had announced the imminent arrival of the kingdom of God, and he had been executed by Roman imperial authorities for treason. And yet, already within the New Testament writings we find a certain ambivalence toward Rome. The Gospels all seem to take pains to exonerate Romans like Pilate in the death of Jesus, laying all the blame upon the Jewish authorities. Paul apparently was imprisoned and executed by Roman authorities, and yet he tells the Romans to "be subordinate to the higher authorities." He continues to say that "whoever resists authority resists what God has appointed," and he thus commands them to pay their taxes and tolls, and pay "honor to whom honor is due" (Romans 13:2, 7).

To be sure, the missionary efforts of the early Christians benefited from the trade networks and roads that Rome had built and the relative tranquility of the Pax Romana, or "Peace of Rome." The Book of Acts would even go so far as to suggest that the empire was a tool of God's providence to benefit the spreading of the Gospel. And yet, the Book of Revelation identifies Rome with the "Whore of Babylon," the pawn of Satan's power in the world. So the question was set from early on: Should Christians, who are citizens of the kingdom of God as it begins to grow on earth, stand opposed to the empire or work within it?

Similarly, from the outside, Roman citizens and authorities were not quite sure what to make of these so-called Christians. Were they a subversive "secret society," or were they yet another of the many new and exotic, but more or less harmless, religious movements that seemed to crop up throughout the empire?

One of the secrets of the success of the Roman Empire was the way in which it was willing to appropriate, or at least tolerate, the culture and religion of those people the Romans conquered or ruled. The official pagan religion of Rome gave obeisance to the traditional pantheon of Olympian gods, with Jupiter at the head. Beginning with Augustus on, the Roman emperor was included in the pagan cult, either as the representative of the gods or as himself divine. But at no time did the Roman cult exclude indigenous religions. Rather, it either tolerated these traditions or incorporated them.

More often than not, the Romans would simply incorporate the gods of conquered peoples into their own pantheon, either claiming that they in fact worshiped the same god under a different name (any god of the sun must be Apollo, for example), or naming the local gods as provincial delegates or bureaucrats for the central government of the Roman pantheon. Strict monotheists like the Jews, however, were not so easy to assimilate, and yet Rome seemed more often than not to respect and tolerate Judaism, until some Jewish leaders encouraged sedition in the revolt of 66–70 A.D. For much of the first three centuries A.D., this sort of benign neglect seems to have extended to Christians too. However, even those inclined to leave Christians alone considered them to be antisocial and superstitious.

Christians were accused of atheism, cannibalism, and libertinism. The charge of atheism arose not simply from the theological differences between the Roman and Christian faiths, but from the practical consequences of those differences. Roman religion was intertwined with Roman politics, as the cult of the emperor makes clear. In addition, to the Romans, empirical evidence seemed to indicate that the Roman cult had given unprecedented prosperity, stability, and peace to the world. The honor paid to the emperor and the gods was simply part of *Romanitas*, "Romanity" or "Roman-ness," the set of habits and practices that made a good, loyal, civilized citizen of the empire. (This is similar to the way respect for "the flag, Mom, and apple pie" used to symbolize the qualities of a good American.) Christians, by rejecting the cult of the emperor in the name of their faith in another god, seemed disloyal to the entire world order that supported them. (The other charges of cannibalism and libertinism probably arose from misunderstandings associated with the Christian practices of Eucharist [eating the Body of Christ] at the agape feast [áh-gá-pay, love feast].) Christianity seemed to many Romans distasteful and unpatriotic. The seeds of conflict were sown, and occasionally they would sprout up.

Traditional, legendary accounts of the tales of the Christian martyrs usually ascribe ten "great persecutions" to the Roman Empire. But modern historical scholarship has found little evidence for these. Some historians, in fact, have suggested that, despite Christianity's valorization of its martyrs, Roman authorities usually acted with tact and discretion in their dealings with Christian dissidents. By this account, Roman actions would be better characterized as "prosecution" of a select few zealots who threatened the peace of the empire. The ancient sources bring no more clarity to the situation. If one reads Christian treatments of martyrdom in the first three centuries, Christian martyrs in the hands of the Romans were engaged in an apocalyptic struggle between the saints and the devil. These "athletes of Christ" wrestled in the arena with Satan himself. Theirs was the choice between confession and denial, between faith and apostasy, between God and "the Adversary." In the Christian martyr's ideal, Rome was simply an instrument of Satan's power.

But many Romans viewed the Christian problem not as a choice between good and evil, but rather between peace and discord. The "atheist" adherents of the Christian sect disrupted the Pax Romana, the "Peace of Rome," in their stubbornness. The Roman response to these troublesome dissidents usually took one of three forms. As I have suggested, it seems that for most of the first two hundred years of Christianity, Roman authorities maintained a policy of limited prosecution by due process. If there was persecution, it was more often than not carried out on a local level, either by imperial successors purging the court of rivals or by local mob activity in isolated provinces, sometimes, but not always, with the support of the local governor. This mob violence grew out of what Robin Lane Fox has called "frustrated Romanity," and is somewhat like the sporadic flare-ups of Christian persecution of Jews throughout the Middle Ages and into the twentieth century. Finally, these first two strategies of response converged in a third, a reactionary imperial reform that systematically persecuted Christians in the late third and early fourth centuries.

Rather than give the details of the many and various persecutions, perhaps it would be better to look at one of the most striking accounts of martyrdom we possess, the *Martyrdom of Perpetua and Felicity*. This account comes from one of the first official actions taken by the Roman government against Christianity around the turn of the third century.

Vibia Perpetua was a "newly married woman of good family and upbringing" (*Martyrdom of Perpetua and Felicity*, #2) in Roman North Africa, in her early twenties and with an infant son. She was a catechumen, and she was arrested with several other catechumens in about 200 A.D. as part of a Roman effort to discourage conversion to Christianity. Among her fellow prisoners was her servant Felicitas. She kept a diary while she was in prison, and it is from this diary that we can see a firsthand account of the nobility and tragic beauty of Christian martyrdom.

Perpetua's tale begins as she is arrested in her home. Her father, who was apparently not a Christian, stands before her and pleads with her to renounce Christianity. She is moved by his plea, but she cannot do what he asks:

> "Father," said I, "do you see this vase here, for example, or water-pot, or whatever?" "Yes I do," said he. And I told him, "Could it be called by any other name than what it is?" And he said, "No."

"Well, so too I cannot be called anything other than what I am, a Christian."

(Martyrdom, #3)

For Perpetua, even before she is baptized, Christianity is essential to who and what she is, and she is willing to face the consequences of that fact.

While in prison, Perpetua receives visions that bring her comfort, foretell her death, and give her confidence that even her death will be a victory for Christ. When after several days her father returns to her, he renews his plea:

> "Daughter," he said, "have pity on my grey head— have pity on me your father . . . Think of your brothers, think of your mother and your aunt, think of your child, who will not be able to live once you are gone. Give up your pride! You will destroy all of us!" This was the way my father spoke out of love for me, kissing my hands and throwing himself down before me . . . I tried to comfort him, saying, "It will all happen in the prisoner's dock as God wills; for you may be sure that we are not left to ourselves but are all in his power."
>
> (Martyrdom, #5)

When she finally comes before the Roman governor, even he seems to take pity on her situation. Before passing judgment, he, too, asks her to reconsider:

> Hilarianus the governor . . . said to me, "Have pity on your father's grey head; have pity on your infant son. Offer the sacrifice for the welfare of the emperors." "I will not," I retorted. "Are you a Christian?" said Hilarianus. And I said, "Yes, I am."
>
> (Martyrdom, #6)

What is so striking here is the intensity and honesty of the emotions portrayed. The father is heartbroken and dumbfounded at her resolve. Perpetua is moved to sadness and pity, but is undeterred. The governor seems reasonable, and even reluctant. And yet the punishment—she was condemned to be mauled to death by wild beasts in the public arena—is brutal, and the delight with which the crowd observes the victims' torture and death is barbaric.

What emerges from this text is both the nobility of the martyrs and the profound confusion that their conviction evokes. One has the sense that both the father and the governor simply do not understand how Perpetua could give up her life over tossing a few grains of incense on the altar of the emperors. The governor enforces his policy, but it seems to be without the gleeful delight of evil that is often portrayed in the movies. Nevertheless, the martyrdom of Perpetua and Felicity is still a public spectacle, and the crowd enjoys their death. So there is a very real face of evil in this account, but it is framed within the elements of "frustrated Romanity" we mentioned before.

This tide of official hostility toward Christianity reached its height in the conservative reforms of the emperors Diocletian and Galerius in 302–310. Feeling threatened on the borders, Diocletian initiated a broad cultural reform to re-invigorate the sense of a common Romanity. But the Diocletian persecution served to demonstrate that the growing Christian movement could not easily be extricated from the structure and routine of Roman life, and Galerius reversed his policy in 311 and issued an edict of religious toleration. The long history of antagonism was drawing to an end.

As we have seen, the opposition between Rome and Christianity was rarely clear-cut, nor was Roman policy often aggressive in the pursuit of Christians. Nevertheless, this painful era of suspicion, isolation, and distrust produced a powerful and persuasive "ethic" of martyrdom. While the survival and continuing growth of Christianity suggest that the great majority of Christians escaped persecution one way or another, the few "athletes of Christ" established a heroic Christian ideal that echoes still in the spirituality of Christians today (see *CCC*, #2473). Ignatius of Antioch's cry that "At last I am made a disciple" as martyrdom approached offered a powerful image of the imitation of Christ, even in death. For Origen of Alexandria, martyrdom was a special kind of death, "Christian, religious, holy." It was an opportunity to share in the work of redemption, and it was undertaken with the conviction that death was already overcome in Christ. Thus, though the persecutions of the Roman Empire were perhaps less aggressive and bloody than previously believed, they nevertheless produced a theology of martyrdom, an ethic of resistance that subordinated the authority of the state to the power of the Reign of God (see *CCC*, #2473).

Drawing the Threads Together: The Birth of the Catholic Church

The first three centuries of Christianity are marked by conflict, both internal and external. This era of the Church was indeed a "baptism of fire." In response to pressures and challenges from those who claimed to be Christians—such as Marcion, Montanus, and the Gnostics—and those who vehemently rejected the Christian faith, such as Jews and Romans, the many and diverse communities of Christians began to draw together into a catholic consensus. By the early 300s, there was an identifiable federation of churches throughout the empire who were united in the essentials of faith, worship, and authority. The churches continued to grow and expand, sinking roots deep into the life and politics of the empire and becoming more and more influential as a political force. While Christians were probably not yet anywhere near the numerical majority in the empire, they could be found in its every corner. They had proven their resilience to Galerius. The opportunity was ripe for a clever politician to make good use of this new broad constituency. That clever politician was Constantine, the first Christian emperor of Rome.

≥≿✝≤≿

For Reflection

1. What connections do you see between the Jewish faith and Catholic Christianity?

2. How would you compare the preaching of the Gospel in the era of "the ethic of martyrdom" and in our present-day Catholic parishes?

CHAPTER 2

Faith Established

As we move into the fourth century, we move from a Christianity that's on the outside of society to a Christianity that's on the inside. That is, Christianity took the first steps on the path toward establishment in the Roman Empire. The year 311 A.D. saw Galerius's edict of toleration; 313 brought the conversion of Constantine as he ascended to the imperial throne and his reaffirmation of tolerance toward Christians in the Edict of Milan. Whether this was a path in the right direction is still a disputed question. Many thinkers, both ancient and modern, have regarded "Constantinianism"—the establishment of Christianity as a state-sponsored religion—as a great disaster for the Church., claiming that Christianity's entrance into the mainstream of imperial culture signified a sell-out of the kingdom of God for the kingdom of this world. Others, however, both ancient and modern, have viewed the conversion of Constantine as evidence of God's providence at work. Even Augustine in his youth would praise the glories of "these Christian times," when Christians could spread the Gospel in a peaceful empire. But the question lingers still: Peace at what price?

Toleration and Its Discontents

When Galerius followed Diocletian to the throne, he initially continued his predecessor's policy against the Christians. But in 311, as his health declined, Galerius apparently had a change of heart. On April 30, 311, he issued a decree:

> After we had decreed that they [the Christians] should return to the institutions of the ancients, many too were completely overthrown; but when most persisted in their determination and we saw that they neither gave worship and due reverence to the gods nor yet could observe their worship of the God of the Christians [since their books had been burned and

their assemblies disbanded], we therefore in consideration of our most mild clemency, and of the unbroken custom whereby we are used to grant pardon to all men, have thought it right in this case also to offer our speediest indulgence, that Christians may exist again, and may establish their meeting houses, as long as they do nothing contrary to order.

(Eusebius, Ecclesiastical History, as quoted in Frend, p. 480)

Galerius died five days later. But with this deathbed pardon, he had begun to shift the course of history. Upon his death, two of the co-emperors, Maximin and Maxentius, tried without success to revive the anti-Christian policy, but they were soon swept under by the tide of a coalition between two of Galerius's rivals, Licinius and Constantine.

Constantine was not a Christian when he began his campaign for the title of Augustus, the high emperor. In 312, just a year before his great victory, he had received a promise of victory and a reign of thirty years from Apollo, the sun god. So why the apparent change of heart? As the story goes, he converted on the battlefield, when in a dream or a vision he saw a cross inscribed with the words "By this sign, conquer." The next day he did just that, overcoming a superior force led by Maxentius at the Milvian Bridge. He entered Rome in triumph, and together with Licinius issued the Edict of Milan in 313. Whereas Galerius's edict two years before had begrudgingly allowed Christians to regather, the Edict of Milan proclaimed religious freedom for all and celebrated worship of the Christian god as first among the other cults of the empire.

But it seems that Licinius and Constantine disagreed on what this prominence meant. Licinius was more or less a Roman conservative, and it seems that he hoped to absorb Christianity into the Roman pantheon. As this seemed less and less plausible, he became more and more hostile to Christians in his court. Thus, when Constantine marched against his former ally in 324, Licinius found himself without the support he needed to resist, and he was defeated. At the battle of Chrysopolis in September of 324, Constantine became sole emperor of Rome.

But was Constantine truly the first *Christian* emperor? Constantine was a warrior to the bone, and in victory he did not hesitate to execute all of Maxentius's family as rivals to his power. His maneuvers against Licinius bear all the marks of a ruthless and devious conqueror, and his reign as emperor is stained with the blood of his own son Crispus, executed under imperial order as a rival to the throne. So his life and conduct are far from saintly. If he was a Christian, he was not a very good one. But then why did such a man sponsor and endow the Christian Church with wealth and honor and take such an interest in its debates over the doctrine of the Trinity? One can see how Constantine may have simply aimed to do with Christianity what Diocletian and Galerius had tried to do with a revived paganism: to draw together citizens from all corners of the empire behind a common purpose and a common sense of identity. When Christianity proved itself vital and resilient in the face of total state opposition, it may have made good sense to make it a friendly force, an ally rather than an opponent. And yet, the tone of Constantine's letters and orations seems to betray a sincere conviction in the providence and grace of the God of Jesus Christ and his own place as God's "servant." Reading his own words, it is hard to believe that Constantine's conversion was utterly superficial.

Whatever Constantine's reasons, whether personal, political, or both, he soon found himself at the head of a great church. While it should be noted that Constantine in no way "established" Christianity in any formal way, the patronage and interest of the emperor in the welfare of the Church should not be underestimated. He immediately began to enfranchise the Church, granting it land and property, raising the clergy to a position of honor and privilege in the empire, exempting them from municipal duties and taxes, and permitting them jurisdiction over some legal matters. In all, Christianity emerged from its disfavor and became central to the civic and the religious life of the empire. The offices of the Church began to be modeled on the offices of the empire, with the Church now adopting some of the bureaucratic structures that had been the key to the empire's efficient operation for centuries. It is perhaps at this point, when the Church becomes Roman as well as catholic, that we can begin to speak of a Roman Catholic Church in any form that we would recognize.

The Search for Purity in a "Lukewarm" Church

Not every Christian shared in the celebration of Christianity's newfound legitimacy. As Christians became more numerous and more prominent in the culture of the empire, a few idealistic believers fled this urbane Christianity into the wilderness. As early as 270 A.D., a young Christian farmer in Egypt named Anthony was sitting at Sunday liturgy when he heard Jesus' command to the rich young man in Matthew 19:21: "If you wish to be perfect, go, sell your possessions, and give the money to the poor, and you will have treasure in heaven; then come, follow me."

These words struck Anthony with powerful force as a message from God to him, and he acted immediately. He placed his sister in a convent, sold all his family property, and moved to the desert regions at the outskirts of his town. Anthony went to the desert in search of a deeper spiritual perfection, and he practiced a strict regimen of fasting and disciplined self-denial to find it.

Eventually, he retreated even farther into the desert, and a community of disaffected Christians hungry for a more rigorous, disciplined life gathered around him, forming a new "city" of ascetics (*askesis* is Greek for "discipline"). He was not the first to find spiritual solace in the desert, but his friend and admirer Athanasius recorded the history of his life, and the story was published throughout the empire. In the wake of Constantine's establishment, hundreds of young men and women imitated Anthony and fled to the wilderness. Christians who had been raised in the martyrs' theology of resistance and self-sacrifice found themselves after Constantine in a world free of persecution, where zeal and commitment were no longer necessary to the faith. For them, the *Life of Anthony* was a manifesto proclaiming the life of Christian excellence and asceticism in the desert regions. In a world without persecution, asceticism offered a life of spiritual martyrdom in the service of God. Under the inspiration of Anthony, the ascetic ideal soon spread throughout the empire, into Cappadocia and Syria and eventually into southern Gaul (France).

North African Christians voiced their discontent with the Constantinian Church in a different fashion. The church in North Africa divided in the early 300s over whether those who had weakly capitulated to the Roman authorities during the persecutions could be readmitted to the fold. Many argued that those who had betrayed the Church could not be readmitted to the body of believers. Such a betrayal was a "sin against the Holy Spirit" (see Matthew 12:31–32) that could not be forgiven.

These rigorous Christians, called Donatists, claimed that they were the true Church of the martyrs and the saints, since only they had maintained the purity and virtue of the Church without the stain of treachery. Their passionate cry for purity in the Church gained a large following and caused enough turmoil to draw the condemnation of Constantine. But the Donatists, convinced of the holiness of their cause, persisted. For a century after, Africa had two parallel churches, each with their own bishops and priests, each with their own basilicas. By the year 400, the Donatist Church was larger in Africa than the Catholic Church, and the Catholic bishops, among them St. Augustine of Hippo, resorted to the use of force to end the schism.

THE ARIAN CONTROVERSY

The Donatists caused only the first such controversy to disrupt the peace of Constantine's empire. In the early 300s, a storm was brewing in Egypt. In 318, Bishop Alexander of Alexandria offered a sermon to his clergy on "Unity in the Trinity." By all accounts, this thorny topic was a bit beyond the reach of

Alexander's theological skills, but one priest in particular disputed the bishop's teaching most aggressively. The priest's name was Arius. It seems that Arius had concluded that if the Logos, the Word of God that had become flesh in Jesus Christ, was said to come "from the Father," then it could not really be God, since "God" was by definition unmoveable and uncreated.

The Word must therefore be a created being, perhaps the first and greatest created being, and to call it "divine" was simply to recognize its supremacy over all other creatures. When Bishop Alexander had insisted on the equal divinity of the Word, Arius took it as an offense against God.

Alexander wrote a letter condemning Arius's teaching in 319, but Arius had the support of other influential figures in the Eastern Church, like the famous bishop-historian Eusebius of Caesarea and his namesake Eusebius of Nicomedia. Very quickly the local dispute in Alexandria had spread across the eastern territories and set bishop against bishop. Constantine, ever seeking to preserve (or discover?) peace in the empire, called for a council of bishops to gather and discuss the problem.

The council was convened in Nicaea, a small town in Bithynia (northern Turkey) near Nicomedia, where Constantine had set up his court. Two hundred twenty bishops responded to the summons, and almost all were Greek-speaking bishops of the East. By the early fourth century, Asia Minor had become the geographical center of the empire, and so only four or five bishops came from the Latin-speaking West. Pope Sylvester I, bishop of Rome, sent two legates rather than attending himself. Even so, this gathering was a momentous occasion, and the participants felt it to be so. In his opening remarks, Emperor Constantine urged the bishops to find unity and peace in the name of Christ. But, according to legend, his words fell on deaf ears as the bishops faced off, pro-Arius and anti-Arius, until Constantine himself proposed that Arius's doctrine be rejected and that the Word and the Father should be considered *homoousios*, of the same essence or being (hence the language in today's Creed, "One in being with the Father," cf. *CCC*, #242). With the weight of imperial authority behind it, this language carried the day, and 218 of 220 bishops signed the creed.

However, while it was clear that Arius's position had been condemned, it was not clear to all what precisely the technical language of "same essence" meant. How specific was the term "same"? Did it refer to exact identity, or to very general likeness? Christian bishops and theologians were now split into several factions, each with their own opinion of how precisely the language of Nicaea applied to God. For a time, it seems, most of the signatory bishops and their successors seemed to retreat from the language of Nicaea, leaving only a few "Nicene" defenders like Athanasius of Alexandria to defend the creed. By the time Constantine died in 337, his son and eventual successor Constantius had taken up the Arian position. The apparent unity of Nicaea had dissolved within a decade.

What was at stake in this debate? It may seem ridiculous that the choice of words about something like the Trinity, which is forever shrouded in mystery anyway, would be worth such a fight. One might suppose at first glance, as indeed many have, that the debate over the Trinity was simply the façade for base political maneuvering. And, to be fair, there were political issues that the participants could not help but draw into the argument. The church in the new capital, Constantinople (what is now Istanbul, Turkey), jockeyed for a place of authority in the universal Church, while the more ancient centers of the faith in Alexandria and Antioch resisted the newcomers. Athanasius, bishop of Alexandria, conceded that Constantinople was important as the new imperial capital, but he insisted that it was not a church established by the Apostles. Certainly, this bad blood between cities couldn't help but influence the arguments about the Trinity.

But the debate cannot be reduced simply to these sorts of political maneuvering. On the Arian side (Arians were the followers of Arius, not to be confused with the Nazi racial term "Aryan"), to say that part of God was "begotten" or "generated" was an offense against the wholeness, simplicity, and perfection of God. God by definition was beyond time and beyond change, and so to call the Word "God" was in a strong sense idolatry, something no good Christian could allow.

On the other side, Athanasius, perhaps the most prolific and obstinate opponent of the Arian revival, argued that faith in Christ's redemptive work itself was at risk. Athanasius argued that the heart of the Gospel is that God saves us. If Arius was right, and if the Word was created, even as the first and highest created being he was still a creature, with the flaws and fallibility of all creatures. The Word in Arius's understanding was not in control of all of God's creation, and so it was impossible to think that a creature could save all other creatures. Only God the Creator can restore creation. To hold the Arian position was to call salvation into doubt. This was a cause to live and to die for, and this was why Athanasius and his party were so obstinate.

When the tide of the debate turned in favor of the Arian position, Athanasius was exiled to the western areas of the empire. In Trier and Rome, Athanasius gained the support of several Western bishops, including the bishop of Rome. For the Western bishops, what was at stake was the proper relationship of the emperor to the Church. No one questioned the authority of the emperor to convene councils, but when he acted to overrule the authority of Rome and Alexandria, he overstepped his authority.

This conflict further alienated the West from the East. Already divided by language and custom, the Eastern and Western bishops were now divided by doctrine. Constantius eventually overcame even his Western opponents, and the empire remained for the most part Arian until his death in 360. But before dying, Constantius made a decision that was to doom the Arian cause. Constantius designated his cousin Julian, who had distinguished himself in battle against the encroaching Germanic barbarians in Gaul (now France) as his successor. Under Emperor Julian, the Arian debate would recede as Christians were forced to unite against paganism's last stand.

Julian, later called the Apostate, had been raised in a Christian family, but he abandoned Christianity long before he ascended to the throne. He was the son of Constantine's half-brother, whom Constantine executed in 337. Then only six years old, Julian was put in the care of the Church and educated in philosophy, literature, and rhetoric. Julian confessed throughout his life that his first and best love was books. It was apparently through his reading of the classics of ancient philosophy that he turned away from Christianity and embraced a pagan mystical philosophy as his religion.

But, for all his love of learning, Julian's path to the imperial throne lay on the battlefield. When Germanic tribes threatened the western territories of the empire in 356, Julian led an army to beat them back. The Persians were pressing at the same time upon the eastern borders, and Constantius turned to his cousin for help. Julian responded with scorn, openly declared his paganism, and began his march to the east to usurp his cousin, not to assist him. Constantius, however, was taken ill with malaria, and on his deathbed, he proclaimed Julian, his erstwhile rival, as his successor.

As emperor, Julian attempted to weed out the Christian Church from the politics of the empire. He first purged Constantius's court of any Christian influence. He then ordered all exiles (including Athanasius of Alexandria) to return to their homes, not out of leniency and tolerance, but rather out of the hope that the rival Christian parties would tear each other apart and leave room for his new paganism. He aimed to revive the pagan priesthoods, temples, and rituals. In essence, Julian attempted single-handedly to reverse the course of progress that Christianity had followed for fifty years or more.

In fact, at times it seemed that Julian may have been motivated more by his hatred of Christianity than his devotion to a particular pagan religion. He issued decrees forbidding Christians from teaching the Greek and Latin classics, and he promoted pagans to prominent positions in his government. He even planned to rebuild the Jewish Temple in Jerusalem, apparently to spite beliefs in that era that the destruction of the Temple was a providential sign of Christianity's superiority to Judaism.

Since he knew Christianity from the inside, his polemic (attack), entitled *Against the Galileans*, was particularly biting. Julian's reign, though lasting less than two years until he fell in battle against the Persians in 363, was a turning point in the Christian world, since it both reminded Christians that their hold upon the power and influence in the empire was by no means secure and turned the tide of the Arian controversy.

Julian himself became a satanic figure in Christian legend, foreshadowing the deceptions and persecutions of Antichrist. And his premature death was taken to be the work of Providence. Some legends even claimed that God had resurrected martyrs to kill him. Ironically, his attempts to eliminate Christianity led to the eventual triumph of Nicene orthodoxy. His predecessors had been clearly Arian and thus had blocked the progress of the Nicene camps. Julian, however, gave equal protection to both Christian sects, hoping that the divisions and in-fighting would lead Christians to destroy themselves from the inside. With space to maneuver, the Nicenes were able to take the first steps toward reclaiming the Church for the authentic teaching of the Council.

Establishment and Collapse: 364–476 A.D.

With Julian's death, the throne passed into the hands of Christian emperors once again. Valentinian became emperor in 364 and split the honor with his brother, Valens. Valentinian took responsibility for the western half of the empire, and Valens became emperor of the East. Valentinian was sympathetic with the Nicene position, and the leaders of the Nicene camp in the West were quick to exploit the opportunity. In a rapid succession of councils in Paris, Rome, and Sicily, priests and bishops convened to condemn the Arian position and those who held to it. Gradually, the tide had turned, and Arian bishops were replaced with Nicenes. Finally, in 373, one of the strongest Arian bishops, Auxentius of Milan, died and was succeeded by an Ambrose, who was only a catechumen but was an ardent Nicene and a governor in the Roman bureaucracy.

Ambrose of Milan was thirty-four years old when he was ordained a priest and consecrated as bishop. Considered one of the four great fathers of the Western Church (with Jerome, Augustine, and Gregory the Great), he set the tone for much of the ancient and medieval Church's approach toward biblical exegesis, liturgical music, and the relationship between church and state. Under his leadership, the Western Church finally extinguished the last sparks of Arianism and became resolutely committed to the Nicene position. Ambrose played a major role in the conversion of Augustine of Hippo and baptized the future saint himself in 387.

The zealous confidence of Ambrose in Church authority led him even to excommunicate Emperor Theodosius I when the latter had rashly ordered the execution of thousands of citizens after a riot in Thessalonica in the year 390. Theodosius's acceptance of the judgment of the Church and his public penance before the people of Thessalonica left a deep impression upon his contemporaries, Augustine of Hippo among the many. (See Augustine's *City of God* V. 26, for example.) With the ever-present influence of Ambrose, Theodosius gradually established orthodox Nicene Christianity as the religion of the empire by issuing laws against heresy and pagan sacrifices in the 380s and 390s. By 397, when Ambrose died, Catholic Christianity had become the sole established religion of the western empire. Almost single-handedly, Ambrose of Milan consolidated and unified the Western Catholic Church.

THE EASTERN CHURCH AFTER ARIANISM: THE CHRISTOLOGICAL CONTROVERSY

The Eastern Church, in the meantime, had also begun to swing in favor of Nicaea. Athanasius of Alexandria died in 373, and the intellectual and spiritual leadership of the Greek-speaking Church passed to three men from Cappadocia, a territory in Asia Minor. The "Cappadocian Fathers"—Basil (the Great) of

Caesarea, his younger brother Gregory of Nyssa, and their friend Gregory Nazianzen—worked to consolidate and clarify Nicene theology in the East. Their efforts culminated in the Council of Constantinople in 381, the second great "ecumenical council" of the Church. The Creed of Constantinople essentially reaffirmed the Creed of Nicaea, with a few expansions. Under the inspiration of Gregory Nazianzen, Constantinople spoke of the Son as "begotten before all time" (or "eternally begotten," as used in the Roman Catholic English translation of the Creed today. See *CCC*, #254–255), and under the inspiration of Basil, the Creed asserted that the Holy Spirit was equal in honor and glory to the Father and the Son, and thus fully divine. ("With the Father and the Son he is worshipped and glorified," in the Creed today. Cf. *CCC*, #685.) With this reaffirmation and clarification, the Council of Constantinople marked the end of the Arian controversy and the first full formal declaration of the doctrine of the Trinity.

No sooner had debates about trinitarian theology settled down, however, when a new theological problem came to the fore in the East: the identity of Christ. The triumph of Nicene theology confirmed that the Logos, the Son of God, was fully divine, but this decision led to the next logical question: How does this divine Son take on human flesh? Again, as with the trinitarian debates, what may seem a fine technical point of theology arose from a very practical concern about the truth of salvation.

On the one hand, it seemed to someone like Apollinaris of Laodicea that, if the Logos were to be able to save humanity, he must be perfect. That meant that he could not be fully human, since humans are fallible and can sin. Apollinaris proposed that the divine Logos had taken the place of the rational human soul in Jesus Christ, so that only the "flesh," the body of a human was taken on. This formulation has become known as a "word-flesh" Christology (*Christology* = "understanding of Christ"). On the other hand, Apollinaris's opponents objected that the Logos somehow had to be fully human, since "what he has not assumed he cannot save."

At the opposite pole to Apollinaris's position was what is called a "word-man" Christology, proposed by Theodore of Mopsuestia, who argued that the Logos "assumed" or "adopted" an individual human person. This idea preserved both the full humanity and full divinity of Christ, but it left unclear whether there was any necessary relationship between the two, and it left open the possibility that there were two persons in Christ, one divine and one human.

Nestorius, the bishop of Constantinople and a follower of Theodore's, sparked a conflict when he rejected the use of the traditional title of Mary as *Theotokos*, "God-bearer" or "Mother of God," in the church of Constantinople, since it seemed to confuse the human person with the divine. Nestorius's subsequent fight with Cyril, bishop of Alexandria, led to a long and vicious debate, never quite as divisive as the Arian controversy but nonetheless serious. Nestorius was condemned and remained so even when a preliminary settlement between his followers and Cyril's was reached at the Council of Ephesus in 431. Like Nicaea a century before, the Council of Ephesus represented the midpoint of the debate, not the end. After Ephesus, a monk named Eutyches proposed that Christ had two natures, one divine and one human, before the Incarnation, but that these two natures were fused into one unique divine/human nature after the Incarnation. Rather than solve the problem, this proposal seemed to complicate the question of salvation even more, since Christ then seemed neither really divine (and thus too weak to save) nor really human (and thus unable to save humanity).

The debate continued for twenty years, even drawing Pope Leo I into the fray, until it was finally settled at the Council of Chalcedon in 451. The formula of Chalcedon, in fact, drew heavily upon Pope Leo's contribution to the discussion in a letter that has come to be known as the *Tome*. It carefully set out the teaching that we understand Christ in two natures, one fully human (vs. Apollinaris) and one fully divine (vs. Arius), without confusion (vs. Eutyches), without separation (vs. Nestorius), and united in one person (vs. Nestorius).

It is important to note that this formula, accepted by both the East and the West, does not really offer a positive definition of how the fully human and fully divine natures fit together. Rather, it sets out the limits of our knowledge (by affirming that this formula is only how "we understand" Christ) and protects that limited knowledge from the excesses of Nestorius, Eutyches, and Apollinaris. Above all, Chalcedon represents the attempt to make sense of and affirm the Gospel of Christ, the message of salvation, in a particular language and culture, with the proper humility.

THE WESTERN CHURCH AFTER AMBROSE: AUGUSTINE AND HIS ADVERSARIES

Although the Western Church was instrumental in solving what is called the Christological Controversy of Ephesus and Chalcedon, most of its theological energies were directed toward other, more local problems. Perhaps the best way to see the many and various controversies and muddles that cropped up in the West in this period is to view them through the eyes of a man who seemed to have his hand in all of them, Augustine of Hippo. Augustine was born in North Africa in 354, and in his youth he was at once very successful and very troubled. His professional success as a teacher of rhetoric in the imperial city of Milan seemed to destine him for the high rank of a provincial governor.

However, by his own account in his *Confessions*, Augustine was persistently restless, spending some time as an adherent of the heretical sect known as the Manichaeans, then converting to Platonic philosophy and finally, at the age of thirty-three, he was baptized into the Catholic Church by Ambrose of Milan. Within a few years of his baptism, Augustine was ordained a priest in the city of Hippo and eventually became its bishop. From this relatively small outpost in the North African countryside, Augustine participated in all the major theological debates of his age.

Augustine's first opponents were his former associates, the Manichaeans. Purported followers of the prophet Mani (d. 276 A.D.), Manichaeans believed that the world was the site of a war between equally opposed forces of good and evil. The forces of good were spirit and light; the forces of evil were in the material world. Like Gnostics, Manichaeans believed that some humans had divine sparks of light trapped within human flesh. Manichaean ritual and practice were devoted to liberating these particles of light from matter so that they could travel along the Milky Way to the heavenly realm of pure Light.

Augustine's early writings were diatribes against the Manichaeans that argued for the goodness of the created world and the sovereignty of God. Augustine argued that evil was not a cosmic power in itself, but rather the rejection of or falling away from the goodness of creation. Although the Manichaeans were numerous and influential in the North Africa of his youth, they gradually disappeared under Augustine's intellectual assault and the increasingly restrictive policies of the state.

Augustine's second great opponent was the Donatist Church. The Donatists survived the official establishment of Nicene Christianity because they were doctrinally orthodox. They were *schismatic*, not *heretical*, since they appointed their own bishops and clergy and rejected the authority of Catholic sacraments, but did not dispute the doctrines of the Church itself. Augustine's writings against the Donatists criticized their strict rigorism and argued that sacraments did not depend upon the moral virtue of the priest or bishop administering them, but rather upon God's grace. He argued very compellingly that the Church was a place for healing of sin from which we all suffer, not for prideful delighting in each other's purity and virtue. This very touching and persuasive argument was balanced, however, by Augustine's support of state suppression—sometimes brutal—of the Donatist Church, so that by the end of Augustine's life, the schismatic Donatists were essentially dissipated.

Augustine's last and perhaps most bitter conflict was one that his own writing provoked. In his *Confessions*, Augustine had acknowledged his struggles with the temptations of sin, both past and present. He was convinced that such temptations could be overcome only with God's assistance, and thus he implored God, "Command what you will, and give what you command."

Pelagius, a zealous preacher from the British Isles who had spent much of his life in Rome, objected to this teaching most vehemently. To Pelagius, this phrase represented a pitiful failure to take responsibility for one's own actions. Pelagius was convinced that God would not issue commands that humans could not fulfill, and thus he asserted that humans could always refuse sin and obey the law. That they did not do so was evidence not of an essential weakness in human nature but of habits and customs deeply ingrained in society.

The debate with Pelagius and his followers led Augustine to formulate and clarify the doctrine that has come to be known as "original sin." Growing out of a strong sense of human weakness and drawing on Paul's Letter to the Romans, Augustine's doctrine claims that human nature itself was damaged by the sin of Adam. Insofar as we were all "in Adam" (see Romans 5:12–21), we are all born with a damaged nature, so that we cannot help but sin. Only through God's grace are we saved from this condition. Recent scholarship has done much to redeem the thought of Pelagius, suggesting that he himself never took his position to the extremes that his followers did. In other words, there is a real question whether Pelagius was in fact guilty of what was later condemned as the "Pelagian" heresy.

Nevertheless, the issues that arose in this controversy made a deep imprint upon Western theology, and the debate has been waged again and again in different forms by Prosper of Aquitaine and John Cassian in the fifth century, by Peter Lombard and Peter Abelard in the twelfth century, and eventually by Martin Luther and his many opponents in the sixteenth century, when it became in many ways the keystone of the Protestant Reformation.

The Church at the End of the Empire

It is perhaps ironic that, just as orthodox Christianity had won its long-fought battle for survival and acceptance in the Roman

Empire, the empire itself began to show real signs of decay or failure. Divisions between the East and the West continued to deepen. With the death of Theodosius in 395, the empire was divided in half between his two sons. The linguistic barriers made any efforts at reconciliation difficult, to say the least. While no formal break was to take place between the Eastern and Western churches for another six hundred years, it became more and more clear that, for both Church and empire, East and West were two separate entities. Thus distanced from each other, East and West each had to turn and face external enemies. Descending upon both halves of the empire from the North was a swarm of Germanic, Slavic, and Asiatic tribes: Goths, Vandals, and Huns, among others. In the East, the Visigoths were just barely thrown off when they attacked Constantinople, and the eastern provinces remained intact, but under constant threat. While Constantinople remained unbowed and unconquered for nearly a millennium, its circle of influence stopped, for the most part, at the borders between those who spoke Greek and those who spoke Latin.

In the West, the Rhine River froze on December 31, 406, and thousands upon thousands of people from Germanic tribes flooded into Western imperial territory. Many were Christians—Arians converted by missionaries in the mid-fourth century—but the bond of faith hardly made the conflict any less brutal. In 410, Rome was sacked by the Visigoths, falling for the first time in eight hundred years. The shock of a fallen Rome spread throughout the empire, leading some Romans even to blame Christianity for the calamities. The concerns were widespread enough to provoke Augustine to write his longest work, the trenchant defense of the Christian worldview called *The City of God*.

But even as Augustine wrote, the situation became ever more grave. Vandals and Goths flooded throughout the empire even into Spain and finally across the Mediterranean into North Africa. When Augustine died in 430, the Vandals stood at the gates of Hippo and soon overran it. And this was only the beginning.

Rome was threatened by Attila the Hun in 452 and sacked again by the Vandals in 455; and these German successors were either Arian or pagan. The western Roman Empire, though it still existed in name, had ceased to be. A new era in the history of the West—and thus in the history of the Catholic Church—was about to begin.

✣

FOR REFLECTION

1. Was Constantine's establishment of Christianity good or bad for the faith? If Christianity gets intertwined with culture and politics, does it make culture and politics better or Christianity worse? or both?

2. Does doctrine matter for ministry? In your opinion, were the people involved in the controversies over the Trinity and Christology just complicating things, or were they trying to clarify the truth of the Gospel?

CHAPTER 3

The Faith of Christendom

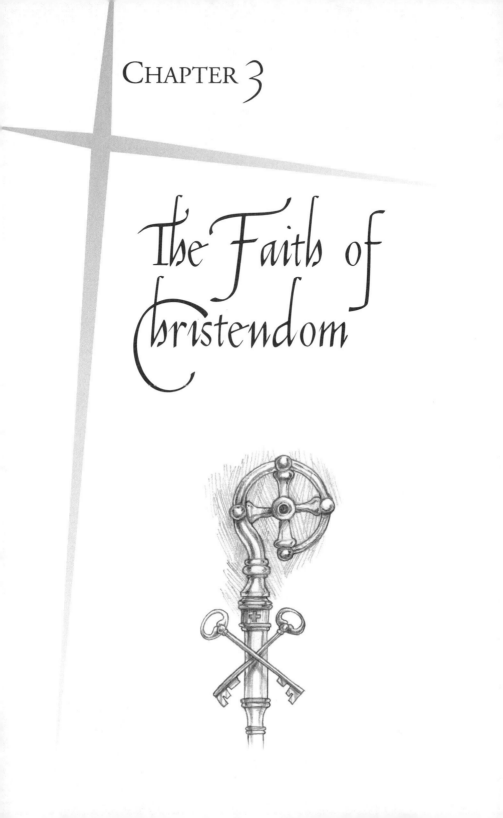

The flood of Germanic tribes into the empire collapsed many of the structures of Roman culture and society. Government, public works, and communication crumbled before the Germanic attack. The only structures that seemed to withstand it were those of the Catholic Church. Catholic bishops represented the faith of the conquered Roman populace now under the control of a German tribal warrior elite that was either pagan or heretical Arian. Could the faith survive in this new and apparently hostile environment? If so, how? This was the challenge faced by the early medieval Church—the fight for survival.

In England, it seemed, the hope for survival initially seemed dim. The Christian Britons retreated before the encroaching pagan Angles and Saxons (hence, "Anglo-Saxon") until they were isolated in the Welsh mountains and left clinging to the far northern coasts of England. On the European mainland, in the earliest stages of the invasions, the mighty warrior kings of the Goths and the Franks found themselves ruling over a majority populace of Catholic Christians. The story of how these two forces, the Germanic and the Roman, the pagan and the Christian, interacted and intermingled is the story of the birth of medieval Christianity, in all its exotic mystery.

The Birth of the Medieval World (500–700): Gregory of Tours and Gregory the Great

One vivid snapshot of this new world in its infancy is found in Gregory of Tours's *History of the Franks*. Gregory of Tours (538–594) was born of a noble Roman family in the territory of northern Gaul. The Franks were among the first of the barbarian tribes to convert to Roman Catholic Christianity, so the conflict between pagan and Christian was never overt in their case. But this is not to say that they suddenly became "civilized" Romans. The Roman Catholicism of sixth-century Gaul is very different from the urbane world of Athanasius and Augustine. Gregory's *History* tells the tale of the Franks' conversion to Western Catholicism, but it also tells of the Roman "conversion," or at least assimilation, to Frankish culture.

Frankish society was based upon the might of the king and the binding ties of tribal obligation. Without a strong king at its center, Frankish political life was fraught with treachery and violence, a world of feuding families and powerful patrons. In such a world, Roman Catholic bishops claimed the supernatural patronage of their saints. These saints, like St. Martin of Tours, acted as the Church's warrior-protectors from beyond the grave, imitating on a supernatural level the social structure of the Franks. Gregory tells of a particular instance where St. Martin protects the monks of his monastery from paying a fine to the local count:

> [A] decree was issued by the judges that anyone who had shown unwillingness to join military expeditions should be fined. The Count of Bourges sent his representatives into one of the religious houses belonging to St. Martin in that region, with orders that the churchmen there should pay the fine. The steward of the house resisted vehemently. "These men serve St. Martin," he said. 'They are not in the habit of taking part in military maneuvers." "This Martin of yours, whom you keep quoting in such a fatuous way, means absolutely nothing to us," they replied. . . . As they said this, one of them marched into the courtyard of the house. He immediately fell to the ground in great pain and became extremely ill. He turned to the steward and said feebly, "Make the Sign of the Cross over me, I beg you, and call upon the name of St. Martin. I full recognize how great is his miraculous power." . . . The steward made a sign to his men and threw the interloper out. From where he lay outside the building, he began to call fervently

upon St. Martin's name. He soon felt better and was cured.

(History of the Franks VII, 42)

According to Gregory, St. Martin could protect his own, as any strong feudal lord would. Full of such stories of miracles and magic, Gregory's *History of the Franks* for us reads like part soap opera and part fantasy novel, and if any period or place in the medieval era counts as a "Dark Age," Gregory's kingdom of the Franks does. And yet it also bears witness to the cultivation of the Gospel in this apparently barbaric culture. When a blood feud breaks out between two warriors, Gregory himself summons them before him and mediates:

> "Men," said I, "you must stop this riotous behavior and not let the wrong which has been done spread any wider. I have already lost several sons of the Church, and I have reason to fear that I may well lose others in this feud. I ask you to keep the peace. Whichever of you has done wrong, let him pay for it in brotherly love . . . . If he who is ordered to pay a fine lacks the wherewithal, the Church will provide it, rather than seek any man lose his soul."
>
> (History of the Franks VII, 47)

The Frankish kingdom could be a cruel, hard, and dark place. But even in the midst of the violence and darkness, the struggle to live out the kingdom of God continued.

Gregory's namesake and contemporary, Pope St. Gregory I (the Great) sheds a somewhat different light upon the life and culture of the late sixth century. Gregory is often said to be the last of the Latin Fathers and the first medieval pope, and in many ways he is a bridge between the Church of Augustine and the Church of the High Middle Ages. Gregory was born in 540 of a wealthy Roman family. The Italy of Gregory's youth had been a battleground: In 533, Justinian, the emperor in Constantinople, mounted a great campaign to reclaim Rome, Italy, and North Africa for the empire. But the Ostrogoths that had settled in Italy for a generation did not give up easily, and although Justinian's armies reclaimed Rome in 563, thirty years of war devastated both armies and the Italian countryside. And to top it off, the imperial armies could enjoy their victory for only a few years before the Lombards—a new, stronger Germanic tribe—swept through Italy and threatened to take Rome, leaving the imperial troops clinging to small territories on the Italian coast.

This was the Italy in which Gregory grew up, a mixed world of Lombard, Roman, and Greek powers, each vying for dominance and influence. Its ties to the East were ties to the imperial past; its daily confrontation with the barbarian culture of the Lombards was evidence of a new and different age. Gregory had been a civil servant, rising to the level of prefect of the city of Rome when he retired in 574 and converted his family estate into a monastic community. In 579, the pope called him out of the monastery to be the papal ambassador to the court in Constantinople. Gregory spent seven years in the East, continually trying to persuade the emperor to assist his native Italy. He returned to Rome in 586 and was elected pope in 590.

Gregory's first task as pope was to assume his old responsibilities for the civil affairs of Rome. Since his retirement fifteen years earlier, Rome's civil administration had collapsed. Gregory reorganized the distribution of food and the civil defense against the always threatening Lombards. He reopened trade between Rome and cities around the Mediterranean. He began to arbitrate civil disputes and judge criminal cases. Perhaps more significantly, Gregory took it upon himself to negotiate a treaty with the Lombards in 592 without the support or permission of the emperor in Constantinople and, when war broke out again in 593, Gregory himself directed the Roman forces. In all these tasks, Gregory was simply taking care of necessities when no one else could.

Nevertheless, this represented in fact an expansion of the responsibilities and authority of the papal office. Since the early years of the Church, Rome had always enjoyed primacy, in part because it was the See (officially the "seat" or "throne" of the bishop) in Rome, the center of the western empire, and in part because it was the last See of Peter, the leader of the Apostles. Gregory extended the responsibilities of his office as the vicar of Peter to include political and administrative tasks previously left to the imperial government. Although Gregory's correspondence with Constantinople shows him to be deferential and respectful of the proper authority of the emperor, he had, in fact, replaced imperial with papal authority in the affairs of the city of Rome and of all of Italy.

Gregory also extended his influence in the churches throughout Europe. He corresponded with bishops and rulers in the Frankish kingdom and in Gothic Spain. He openly rebuked the bishop of Constantinople for taking the prideful title "universal patriarch," arguing that the leaders of the Church should practice greater humility. Gregory preferred his own title, "Servant of the servants of God," which is still occasionally invoked by popes. Perhaps Gregory's most significant intervention into European affairs was his commission of a monk named Augustine to lead a missionary effort in England in 597. The dominant Anglo-Saxon culture of England was virtually untouched by Christianity, but within a century or two, English monks like Alcuin of York would be among the most powerful and influential men in the Catholic Church.

Gregory's pontificate marks the clearest point at which, almost by default, the See of Peter begins to carry both temporal and spiritual authority in the western world. The pontificate of Gregory was the first stage in the centralization of authority and influence in the papal office that was to be one of the hallmarks of the medieval world.

But Gregory's influence did not extend simply to the bureaucratic development of the medieval papacy. To later medieval men, he was "our beloved Gregory," the last of the Latin Fathers. Gregory had the heart of a contemplative, but he knew all too well that the needs of others often required that the contemplative life be integrated with the active life of service. He is one of the first great defenders of this "mixed life" of action and contemplation, which he portrays in his *Pastoral Rule*, still read with interest by pastors and bishops. His *Dialogues* speak of an amazing world of miracles and saints, especially those in and around Rome, not unlike Gregory of Tours's *History of the Franks*. He tells these miraculous tales to assure his contemporaries that God's power and grace were still active in the world, even in the midst of what seemed a dark and evil time. Book II of the Dialogues is of particular interest to our story of the medieval Church, since it is devoted to St. Benedict of Nursia, the author and founder of the Benedictine way of life, to which we will return. In both his political and social accomplishments and his spiritual theology, Gregory the Great represents the seeds, or perhaps even the first fruits, of medieval Christian culture.

THE MONASTIC WORLD OF THE WEST: BENEDICT AND HIS DISCIPLES

As we have said, Gregory devotes the second book of his *Dialogues* to telling the story of St. Benedict of Nursia. Gregory's tale speaks of the miraculous virtues of Benedict, but it is not a biography in our sense of the word and so it is not really reliable as a historical source. Our knowledge of Benedict's life is actually rather sketchy. We know that he was born in Italy in the generation before Gregory's, in ca. 480. He studied in Rome and then experimented with several forms of monastic life before he founded a large monastic community on Monte Cassino, about eighty miles south of Rome, in about 529.

Tradition tells us that Benedict composed the *Rule for Monks* that bears his name. While scholarly evidence cannot support or deny the claim with any authority, the strength of the traditional linkage between Benedict and the *Rule* is strong enough to trust. As we have seen in past chapters, monastic life was born in the deserts of Egypt and arrived in the West with John Cassian about a century before Benedict wrote. Benedict's *Rule* adapts traditions from these other monastic styles, but it is notable for its compassion and moderation, in sharp contrast to some of the ascetic extremes of the Egyptian and Syrian monks. While he does advocate spiritual discipline in the life of a monk— it should be, he says, "a continuous Lent" (*Rule of Benedict* [*RB*] 49.1)—Benedict hopes that in setting up his "school for the Lord's service" he proposes "nothing harsh, nothing burdensome" (*RB* Prol. 46). Benedict has a deep understanding of the human heart—both its virtues and its failings—and is willing to adapt to meet its needs while still persuading it in the love of God. His *Rule* also balances the ideal of personal obedience to a spiritual master, the abbot, with a vision of Christian fraternity and community drawn from Acts 4:32–33:

> Now the whole group of those who believed were of one heart and soul, and no one claimed private ownership of any possessions, but everything they owned was held in common. With great power the Apostles gave their testimony to the Resurrection of the Lord Jesus, and great grace was upon them all.

Benedict thus encourages the brothers to seek that "good zeal which monks must foster with fervent love . . . supporting with the greatest patience one another's weaknesses of body or behavior, and earnestly competing in obedience to one another" (*RB* 72.3–6). This brief document, which Benedict claims is "for beginners" (*RB* 73.8), is one of the most influential documents in Church history.

Benedict's form of the monastic life was one of many models in the sixth century. But over the course of the next few centuries, more and more monasteries adopted the Rule. This gradual consolidation was accelerated in about 800, when Europe was dominated by the family of Charlemagne, the Carolingian dynasty. As the Carolingians worked to unify Europe in politics and culture, the *Rule* seemed a convenient and adaptable tool to draw together the monastic communities throughout the continent. With the reform initiated by Benedict of Aniane (d. 821) and formalized by Emperor Louis the Pious, the *Rule of Benedict* became the sole standard of monastic life in the ninth century. Some scholars have therefore called these early medieval years, from about 600 to about 1000, the Benedictine centuries.

The "Carolingian Renaissance" and the Ideal of Christendom (800–1000)

The legal standardization was just one step taken by the Carolingians to unify European culture and create a new empire. The family of Charlemagne (the name is simply a French contraction for "Charles the Great") had come to prominence in the Frankish kingdom in the 670s, just at the time when the recently converted Anglo-Saxons in England began to send missionaries to the outskirts of the kingdom in France and Germany. The greatest of these Anglo-Saxon missionaries was named Wynfrid, but he is known to most of us as St. Boniface. Boniface worked from about the turn of the year 700 until his martyrdom among the Frisians, yet another Germanic tribe, in 754. His tireless missionary work led later medieval people to call him The Apostle to the Germans. The Carolingians supported the work of these missionaries, since their work could in fact aid in the consolidation of Carolingian rule over these border territories.

But the strongest force pulling the Carolingian empire together came from outside its borders. From the deserts of Arabia in the early 600s arose the sirocco windstorm of Islam. The crusading Muslims swept over the Mediterranean coast lands of North Africa with almost universal success, engulfing the rich Christian culture that had nurtured Church fathers like Tertullian and Augustine. In 711, they crossed from North Africa into Spain and conquered the Visigothic kingdom. Their progress continued steadily up through the Spanish territories and into France as far as Poitiers. It was there that Charles Martel, the Carolingian warrior king, repelled the Muslim invaders and halted their progress into Europe. Charles, of course, was a hero, and his victory became one of the mythical touchstones of French history. His place as "savior of Europe" allowed him to extend his kingdom over the territory the retreating Muslims left behind.

In addition, his status as the defender of Christianity further solidified the resolve of the papacy to support the Carolingian dynasty. Charles's son, Pepin, was anointed as "king of the Franks" by St. Boniface at the pope's behest. While he was already king by right of inheritance, this ritual anointing invoked the glories of King David in Israel and gave a certain holy authority to the king. Together, the papacy and the Carolingian family were building and extending a new empire.

The new empire found its emperor in Charlemagne, Pepin's son. Charlemagne continued his family's program, and he maintained the close ties they had established with the papacy. On Christmas Day in 800, Charlemagne was in Rome. As he knelt at the end of Mass, Pope Leo III placed a crown upon Charlemagne's head, apparently without warning the king that he was going to do so. The Roman clergy cried out, "Charles Augustus, crowned great and peace-giving emperor of the Romans, life and victory!" Taken by surprise, Charles the Great had become the first Roman emperor in over three centuries.

To a certain extent, the coronation simply confirmed what was already the case. Charlemagne had conquered most major rivals to his reign and had extended his realm over much of France, Germany, and Italy, and he had accomplished this with the full cooperation of the papacy. Crowning Charlemagne endowed this unofficial partnership with a sense of sanctity, legitimacy, and tradition: Charlemagne was the new Constantine. And yet the ninth century was a different world, and Charlemagne's vision of empire was fundamentally different. The geographic center of the empire had shifted north to Germany, but the cultural center was different, too. Charlemagne's aids, especially Alcuin of York, had begun even before the coronation to speak of Charlemagne as the king of a "Christian empire"— "Europa," the realm of Latin Christianity. Far from a renewed Roman Empire in the west, thinkers like Alcuin envisioned a new unified Christian culture and society. The ideal of Christendom was born.

Talk about "Christendom" has fallen out of fashion in recent years. Perhaps for good reason, we have begun to doubt that the Gospel could truly be integrated into politics, culture, and society, and we tend to protect the separation between "church" and "state" as the best possible solution. So perhaps it is difficult for us to imagine the daring proposition put forth by Alcuin, suffused with the hopes that a truly Christian culture and society were possible.

If Church history is in fact the story of discipleship, of the attempt to live the life of the Gospel in particular times and places, then the Carolingian renaissance is one such attempt on a grand scale. Under Charlemagne, the intellectual world was reborn. Benedictine monasteries at Auxerre, Lyons, and Rheims, and throughout France and Germany became centers of learning where scholars sought to synthesize the teachings of Augustine and Jerome, of Ambrose and Gregory, into a unified Christian wisdom. Canon law and biblical study became cornerstones of a system of Christian education. The Carolingians even developed a new standardized book-script that was legible and easy to use for all, so that scholars and politicians could communicate across the empire with ease.

The project was ambitious, and perhaps doomed to failure. In a fallen world, it is hard to imagine a culture and society that is really suffused with the Gospel of Christ. Even the political unity established by Charlemagne could not survive his death. But, given its ultimate failure, the Carolingian renaissance accomplished some remarkable feats of culture and learning, and the ideal of a united Christendom became part of the medieval vision that lasted until the Reformation of the sixteenth century.

The Gregorian Reform (1050–1120): The Pope as Abbot to the World

Charlemagne's empire crumbled after his death, when his sons and their sons divided and subdivided Europe into several monarchies. Split as they were, the kingdoms were further reduced by the recurring waves of Vikings assaulting the shores of Europe and Britain from about the mid-ninth century on. Hopes for the political and cultural unity of Europe died. But the Christendom ideal survived. In the eleventh century, it was revived in the papal court by a group of radical Benedictine monks. This small band of men began what is usually called the Gregorian Reform, and what one scholar has called a world revolution.

After a century of decline after Charlemagne, the embers of the monastic ideal of Benedict were fanned into flame with the foundation and expansion of the Abbey of Cluny in France in the tenth century. Cluny and its numerous daughter houses pursued an intensified observance of the Rule of Benedict. In particular, Cluniac monks were known for their elaborate liturgies and took on the role of intercessors for the Christian kings who supported them. Their vitality and zeal overflowed to inspire the world of the laity. The early eleventh century saw committed Christian kings like St. Edward the Confessor and Henry III of Germany, who was called the emperor monk. Nobles throughout Europe took oaths to commit themselves to just warfare or peace and to refuse to fight on holy days in the Peace of God movement that spread across the continent in the 1050s. The hum of change and reform rippled throughout the Christian world, awaiting someone to channel it. The task fell to a small band of enthusiastic monks in the papal court.

The first important reforming pope in this period was Leo IX (1049–1054). Leo was committed to reforming the clergy in the Church, since the sins of simony and concubinage were widespread. *Simony*, named for Simon Magus, the notorious pseudo-apostle from the Book of Acts, is the practice of buying or selling Church offices—a sort of Church-level bribery. A *concubine* is a live-in sexual companion outside of marriage. For Leo, these practices were symbolic of a host of clerical abuses, and he aimed to stop them. Leo IX, much like John Paul II and other reforming popes, traveled widely across the Christian kingdoms, becoming a visible sign of spiritual authority in the various kingdoms he visited.

According to one account we possess, Leo could be very persuasive on these trips. At the Synod of Rheims in 1049, Leo was presiding over a procession to move the relics of St. Remigius to a new location when the pope halted the procession halfway through, contrary to plan, and had the relics placed upon the altar. Turning to the stunned bishops and clergy, with the holy relics in full display, Leo invoked the holy witness of St. Remigius and asked each bishop and abbot to declare whether he had paid any sum for his office. A murmur spread throughout the crowd, and several in attendance asked for a private meeting with the pope, away from the prying eyes of public scrutiny. Several bishops repented, a few were deposed, and one disappeared in the middle of the night, apparently too afraid to admit his sin. At the end of the session, Leo picked up the body of St. Remigius and bore it on his shoulders to its shrine. Through such dramatic and spiritually charged appeals, Leo IX made the papacy a vibrant, visible, powerful source of public moral exhortation and spiritual leadership throughout the Western Church.

As he traveled around Europe, Leo gathered a small band of like-minded reforming monks. Among these were Hildebrand, Humbert, and Peter Damian, the three key figures in what came to be known as the Gregorian Reform. With a deep hatred of simony, these three exhorted the clergy to "spiritual poverty" and to a return to the "holy, simple life of the primitive Church." This exhortation was, above all, a call for the Church to extract itself from the tangled network of medieval politics and economics. Simony allowed wealthy nobles to "acquire" an archbishop by buying the office for one of their kinsmen. Priests with concubines often had children, and by medieval law these children had certain rights of inheritance. It was for this reason, to remove clergy from the politics of marriage and inheritance, that the religious authority of priestly celibacy was emphasized and enforced. Like the Cluniac monks a century before, these "Gregorian" monks tried to separate the spiritual pursuits of the Church from the obligation to any lay noble or lord.

Humbert, the cardinal archbishop of Silva Candida, was the most radical and cantankerous of the major reformers. He went so far as to suggest, like the Donatists, that the sacraments administered by a bishop who had gained his position through simony were invalid. Humbert was also a papal delegate to Constantinople under Leo IX, and he was responsible for the first formal break between the Eastern "Orthodox" and the Western "Catholic" churches. As a radical reformer, Humbert was perhaps the worst person to send to the East, where the emperor still acted as head of the Church. It is perhaps in reaction to this close alliance of clergy and imperial politics that Humbert excommunicated the patriarch of Constantinople, who in turn excommunicated him. Humbert was by all accounts a zealous and difficult person. The Great Schism that he began in 1054 remains one of the darkest legacies of the reform movement.

Other reformers, such as Peter Damian, were more moderate, but even he encouraged the laity to turn away so-called "simoniac" priests. "Spiritual poverty" for the Gregorians was both a legal and a spiritual concept of reform. Spiritually, it was a call to moral purity and repentance, while legally it was the systematic attempt to separate the Church from lay control. As the movement progressed, the legal dimension of reform became more and more prominent, but the spiritual dimension was never lost. The movement climaxed when Hildebrand the monk was elected pope and took the name Gregory VII, from which we get the term "Gregorian reform." The thrust of Gregory's reform came to rest upon the rather technical legal issue of "lay investiture."

It was customary that the king or emperor, a layman, would have the right of "investing" a newly appointed bishop in his kingdom with the ring and staff that were the symbols of his office. Since the king could refuse to do so, this practice gave him a "veto" over the Church appointments, an important "check and balance" for a king to possess when bishops inevitably became powerful political figures within their realm. However, for Gregory VII, lay investiture implied that priestly authority was subordinate to royal authority, and he rejected the implication. For Gregory, the spiritual power of the Church was superior to the temporal power of the king and, indeed, so "full" was the pope's power as head of the Church that he could even depose the emperor. This led to a long protracted conflict with Henry IV, the "Holy Roman Emperor " (titular heir of Charlemagne) and king of the Saxon lands in eastern Germany. The conflict climaxed in the famous spectacle of Henry standing barefoot in the snow at Canossa in January of 1077 to repent and seek reconciliation with the Church. The controversy did not end there, however, and Gregory ended his papacy and died in exile, chased from Rome by Henry's troops.

After Gregory, the reform movement took a different turn. His successor, Urban II, consolidated and streamlined papal government and, perhaps more significantly, called the First Crusade in 1095. Like the Great Schism, the Crusades are a dark legacy of the Gregorian reform, but it is important to see them within that context. Gregory VII's papal court had become embroiled in the politics of Europe and, despite his intentions to the contrary, it became, in effect, just another contending power among powers vying for allies and influence. Far from lifting the Church out of politics, Gregory had pressed it deeper into the political web. By calling the Crusade to reclaim the Holy Land, Urban invoked the spiritual authority to give the call to the heads of state and acted as the leader of a united Christendom, attempting almost by an act of will to unite Europe in a common task under the spiritual authority of the papacy. At the Council of Clermont, Urban II stood before the assembled bishops of France and Germany and lamented the loss of Jerusalem and the dissolution of the Greek Christian empire under the onslaught of Muslim invaders. He called upon all the "Franks," both French and German, to unite and avenge these attacks upon Christianity:

> Let those who have formerly been accustomed to contend wickedly in private warfare against the faithful fight against the infidel, and bring to a victorious end the war which ought already to have been begun. Let those who have hitherto been robbers now become soldiers. Let those who have formerly contended against their brothers and relatives now fight against the barbarians as they ought. Let

those who have formerly been mercenaries at low wages now gain eternal rewards. Let those who have been exhausting themselves to the detriment both of body and soul now strive for a twofold reward.

(Urban II, *Sermon to the Council of Clermont*, as reported by Fulcher of Chartres, 1095)

Urban's sermon offers the Frankish warlords a virtuous and noble cause, not on behalf of their own political or material wealth, but on behalf of all Christendom. The call to the Crusade is thus a sort of exhortation to conversion to the true mission of Christian society. The First Crusade is a Gregorian movement to the core and, as one historian has commented, truly expresses "all that was highest and lowest in medieval society."

Like any great movement or "world revolution" in history, the Gregorian reform left a mixed legacy to the medieval world. The Gregorian vision had sought to spiritualize and purify the Church. To the Gregorians, only this strengthened spiritual Church was equipped to order the rest of society into a real *Christianitas*, a true Christendom. The Gregorians were monks, and their model of reform was monastic, with attention to order and obedience. In effect, the Gregorian reform was an attempt to "monasticize" the world, and this required obedience to the spiritual authority of an abbot, the pope.

To say whether the Gregorian reform was successful or not depends on your perspective. On the one hand, the specific reforms of Gregory VII ended in compromises that could never have satisfied the zealous pope. And yet, with respect to its broader aims of "spiritualizing" society, the reform must be counted as at least partially successful. The zeal of the reformers transferred to society and sprouted up throughout the twelfth century both as vigorous reform movements and popular heresies. Unfortunately (and perhaps inevitably), these reforming movements often met a hierarchy poorly equipped to deal with their zeal. But the Gregorian reform lies at the roots of so much of what is called the renaissance of the twelfth century.

The High Middle Ages (1100–1300): The Flowering of Religious Life and the Birth of Scholasticism

The Gregorian reform had breathed the winds of change into medieval society at the end of the eleventh century. The spirit of reform swept throughout Europe and inspired new and experimental forms of religious observance, while it also kindled the sparks of learning in some of the traditional monastic and cathedral schools. In the wake of the Gregorian ideal, the late-eleventh, twelfth, and thirteenth centuries saw the founding of the Cistercians, the Carthusians, the Augustinian Canons, the Franciscans, the Dominicans, and a host of other smaller orders, all of which brought new life and fresh insight to the religious life and leadership of the Church. In addition, the twelfth century witnessed incredible intellectual growth, both in the new rigor of an intellectual method called scholasticism, which was represented by scholars like Anselm of Canterbury and Thomas Aquinas, and in the visionary monastic theologies of people like Bernard of Clairvaux and Hildegard of Bingen. The twelfth century was perhaps the most fertile cultural era between the Roman Empire and the famous Renaissance of Da Vinci and Michelangelo.

Gregory VII and his friends had called the clergy to return to the "holy, simple life of the primitive Church," and in a sense the flowering of religious life in the twelfth century represents many attempts to answer this call to return to what medieval religious thinkers called the *vita apostolica*, the "apostolic life." For the Cistercians (named for the Latin name of their first monastery at Citeaux in France), this answer came through a return to the ancient ascetical rigor of the *Rule of Benedict*. Cistercians believed that Benedictine life had become too lax and worldly. The monks of Cluny had accumulated great wealth and spent most of their day in elaborate and splendid liturgies. The Cistercians advocated a return to the simplicity of Benedict's *Rule*, observed literally, without adaptation. They wore white habits to symbolize their commitment to the purity of monastic life. This rigorous order of monks grew rapidly in the early twelfth century, initially in houses of men only, although later women's houses were added. The Cistercians produced some of the great monastic theologians of the twelfth century, above all St. Bernard of Clairvaux, the "Mystical Doctor." They are the spiritual ancestors of the Trappists, most famous now as the order of Thomas Merton and Thomas Keating.

The Augustinian canons reached back even farther into the tradition, beyond St. Benedict to St. Augustine and to the Apostles themselves for their model of the religious life. Unlike the Cistercians, the Augustinian canons decided not to flee the world but to serve it directly. The early Augustinians revived a sense of apostolic mission, of evangelization and service to society, in their vision of the *vita apostolica*. They usually settled in or around towns and cities in small, modest communities, performing for the small landowner or townsperson the same services of intercession, service, and burial that the Benedictines had rendered to the greater nobility for centuries. Perhaps their best-known leader in their early years was Norbert of Xanten, a dynamic and popular preacher. His religious house at Premontre gave his small section of Augustinian canons their name, the Premonstratensians. In the twentieth century, they are often found under the name of their founder, the Norbertines.

Perhaps the most significant legacy of this renewal of the religious life in the twelfth century was the new movement of mendicant friars, the Dominicans and the Franciscans. Extending the insight of the Augustinians into the apostolic mission of disciples, Dominicans and Franciscans lived in the cities and towns as well. However, they lived the life of mendicants, or beggars, living in total poverty, possessing nothing. St. Dominic founded his "Order of Preachers" (hence the "O.P." after a Dominican's name) to preach to the laity against heresy. Poverty was for Dominic a means to an end: it kept his friars (or "brothers") free to pick up and move where they were needed without having ties and commitments to particular places. For Francis, on the other hand, poverty seemed to be almost an end in itself, the perfection of the life of the Gospel. For Francis, Christ and the disciples had been poor wanderers with "nowhere to lay their heads." He and his brothers aimed to imitate this life literally, "without gloss" (cf. Francis's *Testament*). Together, the Franciscans and the Dominicans became the shining lights of the Church in the thirteenth century, each producing their own scholastic giant—St. Bonaventure from the Franciscans and St. Thomas Aquinas from the Dominicans.

The growth of these formal, recognized orders of religious was accompanied by an informal movement around Europe of women called *beguines*. Beguines were lay women who took no formal perpetual vows, observed no formal rule, and sought no recognition from Rome but who lived in community houses centered on a life of prayer and continued to work in the world. As one can imagine, this apparently spontaneous movement among devoted lay women did more than raise an eyebrow in the clerical hierarchy, and indeed a few beguines were burned at the stake for heresy. But these communities of women also produced a rich spiritual legacy of their own in a lay or "vernacular" theology (since few if any of these women wrote in Latin) that we can see in the writings of Hadewych and Mechtild of Magdeburg, and which we are only now beginning to recover.

In addition to, and sometimes in tandem with, all these rich developments in the religious life were equally rich developments in the intellectual world of theology. St. Anselm of Canterbury is usually credited as the "Father of Scholasticism" for the ways in which he integrates the rigors of philosophic analysis with a deep reading of the theology of the fathers of the Church.

The "scholastic method" was a staged process of reflection and organization of thought upon theology. Its first step was *lectio*, careful reading, usually of the Scriptures, with attention to details of grammar and meaning of words. This was followed by the *quaestio* or "question," inquiring into specific problems that arise out of one's reading and bringing philosophy and theology to bear upon them. After this came *disputatio*, engaging in critical conversation with fellow scholars over the argument set out in the question. Then the process culminated in the *summa*, the summary or synthesis of the results of the process in a rational and coherent order. But the last stage was always *praedicatio*, preaching and teaching with clarity and precision. So, despite its often detailed and seemingly obscure turns of phrase, scholasticism always had a practical end in mind. This method had many masters, but the two most famous in the Catholic tradition are St. Thomas and St. Bonaventure, the Dominican and the Franciscan, evidence that the two strands, the intellectual and the religious, were synthesized and integrated in the thirteenth century.

The twelfth and thirteenth centuries are often celebrated in Catholic circles as the apex of Christian civilization and culture. One Catholic author even dared to call his study of this period *Thirteenth: The Greatest of Centuries*. Such praise may be a slightly enthusiastic exaggeration, but one cannot deny that this period was among the most creative and inspiring in the times that we have surveyed. If "Christendom" was never to be a political or social reality in Europe, perhaps this period does show how close indeed western Europe came to a multinational synthesis of Christianity and culture. Unfortunately, it was not a synthesis built to last.

❧✚❧

FOR REFLECTION

1. What does the term medieval mean to you? Dusty old stuff? Primitive barbarians? Wizards and dragons? Is the world of the medieval Church at all like our own? How?

2. How does the *vita apostolica* look today? Are there groups around us that are living witnesses to this passion for the "apostolic life"?

CHAPTER 4

Faith Divided

The medieval synthesis was not built to last. The idea of reform that led to the synthesis was ultimately the source of its own undoing. The papacy of the high and late Middle Ages remained deeply influenced by the Gregorians in two ways. First of all, the papacy continued to develop its institutions, laws, and bureaucracy, centralizing Church authority more and more in Rome. But secondly, the conflict begun by Gregory VII between the papacy and the emperor of the Germans continued on into the twelfth century, until an agreement was reached in 1122, and it was soon echoed by conflicts on the same sorts of issues between Rome and the kings of France and England.

Papal Authority in Crisis: The Avignon Popes and the Great Papal Schism

The desire of the Gregorians to "spiritualize" the authority of the Church, to lift it out of the partisan politics of the medieval monarchies, was repeatedly lost in the irony that had plagued Gregory himself: The popes of the 1100s and 1200s remained embroiled in the political battles of Europe. Innocent III was perhaps the most effective of these popes, and his success was due in part to his Gregorian sense of authority. Innocent did not claim explicit authority over the political legitimacy of kings. Rather, he acted in his capacity as the spiritual leader of all Christians, including monarchs. His claim to authority was therefore pastoral, not political, even if his actions had political consequences.

The least successful of the medieval popes, on the other hand, failed to make this distinction. Boniface VIII, by all accounts a reckless and aggressive person, made grander claims for papal authority than any of his predecessors. His "bull," or papal declaration, of 1302, entitled *Unam sanctam*, declared boldly and unequivocally that the spiritual power of the papacy holds jurisdiction over the temporal power of kings. Boniface issued this bull in the midst of controversy with the king of France, apparently thinking that such a forthright declaration from the Vicar of Christ would silence the opposition. His "strong-arm" claims backfired upon him when the French king responded by sending his troops to capture and imprison the pope in 1303. Although Boniface was soon released, the strain of imprisonment had been too much and he died three days later.

This French victory over the papacy shifted the balance of power in the Church. In 1305, a French-speaking bishop was elected pope. Rather than traveling to Rome, the new pope asked the college of cardinals to meet him in Lyons. He was consecrated pope there in the French countryside, and he and the cardinals took up residence in nearby Avignon. This small town on the frontiers of France remained the home of the papacy for the next seventy years. Later scholars would call this the Babylonian captivity, invoking the Old Testament story of the leaders of conquered Israel who were forced to live in Babylon. In fact, the Avignon papacy still continued to play a significant role (usually a role friendly to France, of course) in the affairs of Europe. But the Roman Catholic Church had, in one sense, ceased to be Roman.

To many Catholics, the pope's absence from Rome was a scandal. Rome, after all, was the See of Peter, and Peter's successor should reside there. Two of the most outspoken and persuasive voices in favor of the pope's return were St. Catherine of Siena, the fiery young Dominican, and St. Bridget of Sweden. Both women were visionaries who had traveled around Europe on preaching tours and gathered tremendous followings. Through their letters and exhortations, they finally prevailed upon Pope Gregory XI to return to Rome.

Unfortunately, the solution to one problem became the beginning of another. Gregory had returned to find the people of Rome deeply resentful of French-speaking people like him, and from time to time, mobs threatened violence in the streets of Rome. When Gregory died the year after he returned, the election that followed his death was attended by only sixteen cardinals. Eleven of these were French, four were Italian, and one was

Spanish. From within the conclave, the cardinals looked out upon chaos in the city of Rome. Riots broke out right outside the conclave walls when the rumor spread that there would be another French pope who would return to Avignon. So despite the heavy French contingent, the cardinals, perhaps out of fear, elected an Italian to become Pope Urban VI. Narrowly escaping the city with their lives, the twelve non-Italian cardinals retreated to Anagni, a town in Italy out of reach of the Roman mobs, and declared Urban's election invalid several months later. They claimed that the election had taken place under duress. When asked why he had held his tongue for several months, one cardinal insisted that "if the pope or other Romans found out that I or some other member of the sacred college had doubts about his election, none of us would escape." They held another conclave and elected another pope, Clement VII, who soon returned to Avignon. With two popes, one in Rome, the other in Avignon, the "Great Western Schism" had begun.

Which one was the true pope? The Church at that time found it difficult to say. The major political powers quickly sided with whichever pope best suited their needs: England and most of the German empire, the major rivals to France, sided with Urban in Rome; France, Scotland (which was struggling for independence from England), and the Spanish king preferred Clement in Avignon. Even the saints of the time could not agree. St. Catherine of Siena favored Rome; St. Vincent Ferrer, Avignon. From the historical evidence, it is nearly impossible to decide who was really the successor to Peter. If both claims to apostolic succession were in doubt, one thing was certain: *the unity of Western Christendom was dead.*

The schism fractured the structure of papal government that had been built since Gregory VII. The Roman pope had no bureaucratic infrastructure, since most of the cardinals had sided with Avignon. He was forced to live hand-to-mouth on the quick money that came from the sale of indulgences, offices, and land. In Avignon, the bureaucracy was still in place and working well, but the pool of taxable territories had been cut by more than half.

The curia at Avignon therefore more than doubled the tax burden upon its own loyal followers, gradually undermining the very bedrock of their support. Each side attempted to overcome the other through force of arms, but neither made any progress. So far from the Gregorian vision, the papacy (papacies?) had become a card to be played in the European game of royal rivalries and partisan politics.

When the Church had faced crisis and division in the past, general councils had been called to solve them, as in the Arian controversy in the days of Athanasius. With this fact in mind, several prominent leaders in the Church tried to call a council that would have authority over the popes. But the notion of papal authority had developed since Nicaea, and the notion that a council of assembled bishops could overrule a pope was controversial, to say the least. When these prominent leaders, called *conciliarists*, convened a council at Pisa in 1408, they only succeeded in dividing the Church further. The bishops at Pisa deposed both popes and elected another, hoping that the crisis would then come to an end. But in Avignon and Rome the council's decree was ignored, which left *three* popes to contend for loyalty *and* a committed band of conciliarists still claiming to have authority over all of them. This swirling anarchy finally ended at the Council of Constance in 1414. The fathers at Constance first discussed the canonical justification for conciliarism, very carefully avoiding an immediate action toward any of the contending popes. By delaying the confrontation, the Council was able to allow its pressure to work subtly on the popes, so that all three eventually resigned or were deposed. Only then was a new pope elected. The Great Western Schism had ended.

Restoration or Reform? Papal Indulgence and Lay Piety

In the hopes of preventing another schism in the future, the Council fathers at Constance had issued a decree called *Frequens* which scheduled general councils to be called in 1423, 1430, and then every ten years thereafter. The document declared that if a given pope refused to call a council, it was appropriate for one to convene without his summons. If another schism erupted, a council would convene within a year, again without any summons. In one sense, the provisions were conservative. Having felt the sting of schism, the Council fathers sought to preserve the unity of the Church and the integrity of the papal office. But, in effect, these changes were revolutionary, to say the least. For the first time, the Church had developed canonical provision for regular checks and balances upon papal authority, and this seemed to question the "fullness of authority" that popes had claimed as their right for centuries.

But the tradition of the papacy had deep roots in the Western Christian psyche. Within a few years, as the memory of the schism retreated and the popes remained in power without division or controversy, most of those who held the conciliarist position moved more and more towards favoring the authority of the pope, leaving only a few radical conciliarists to cling to the position of Constance. By 1460, conciliarism was dead and the pope had re-established his authority over the Christian churches. If substantive reforms of Church institutions were to come, they would have to come from the papacy. Unfortunately, it was just at this point that the papacy seemed least prepared to take on the responsibility of reform.

After a long absence from Rome, a succession of popes in the fifteenth century set about the project of restoring the splendor of the papacy in the See of Peter. The so-called Renaissance popes were known for their lavish lifestyles and worldly indulgences. As the story goes, Pope Leo X after his coronation pronounced with satisfaction, "God has given us the papacy; now let us enjoy it!" Innocent VIII, without shame or embarrassment, proudly and publicly celebrated the marriages of his illegitimate daughters with lavish banquets on the lawn of the Vatican palace. (Of course, to be fair, it is due to these spendthrift popes that today we can enjoy the grand opulence of St. Peter's Square, the Sistine Chapel, and other wonders of the Vatican.) The papacy of these years was focused intensely upon its local domain of Rome and the surrounding papal states and had little time or attention for the calls to reform that were breaking out throughout the Catholic Church.

For break out they did. The fifteenth and sixteenth centuries saw vibrant reforms in the spiritual life of the religious and the laity. As we've seen in previous chapters, reform in spirituality is often expressed in new forms of the religious life, inspired by a particular idea or charism. For the Cistercians, it was a rigorous return to the austerity of the *Rule of Benedict*; for the Franciscans, it was the life of poverty. The new forms of the spiritual life that began in the twelfth and thirteenth centuries had brought spirituality closer and closer to the everyday lives of the laity. The Augustinian canons lived in their own house and prayed together, but were in and around a town, unlike the traditional Benedictine isolation. Franciscans made the spiritual life even more visible, since they depended for their food and shelter upon the benevolence of lay folks. And Francis even founded a "lay order" of Franciscans, the so-called Third Order, to accommodate those who wished to live their lives of work and family with the guidance of Franciscan principles. Finally, the beguines of the thirteenth century were themselves lay women, working in the world, who had chosen to live in community with other women. This movement toward the life of the laity continued in the fifteenth and sixteenth centuries.

But, of course, the laity had a spirituality all along. Lay folks from all walks of life attended the liturgy, supported the monasteries, received the sacraments, and so on. If spirituality is the lived expression of faith, then of course any member of the Church has some form of spirituality, whether explicit or implicit. The difference that we see in the late Middle Ages is that the spirituality of the laity is more explicit, more self-conscious, and perhaps more innovative and critical of traditional religious practices than before.

Perhaps the best-known of these movements of lay piety in the later Middle Ages was the so-called Modern Devotion, *Devotio moderna*, which spread through the Netherlands in the fifteenth century. Founded by Geert Groote in the mid-1300s, the Modern Devotion sought to bring the intensity of religious observance to men and women who had not taken formal perpetual religious vows. In this way, the Devotional ideal was similar to that of the beguines years before. Groote's Brothers and Sisters of the Common Life observed a near-monastic combination of intense individual prayer and shared community life. A priest associated with the movement, Thomas à Kempis, composed one of the most popular devotional classics ever written, the *Imitation of Christ*. The *Imitation* paints a vivid picture of what we might call the medieval ethic of holiness, the conviction that in order to stand before a holy God we must ourselves be holy. Life on earth was therefore a process of purification through penance and prayer. Thomas combines this traditional ethic of holiness with a renewed focus upon the individual, leading one scholar to claim that he shows the "individualism of the age taking its appropriate form in Catholic spirituality" (Evennett, p. 36).

Another dimension of reform "in the members" of the Church was what we usually call Christian humanism. The later Middle Ages saw the rediscovery of the Greek and Latin classics—in what we usually call the Renaissance—and with this revival came a newfound passion for the ancient sources of the Christian tradition. Scholars like Erasmus of Rotterdam and St. Thomas More were deeply entrenched in the study both of the classical authors and the Scriptures and Fathers of the Church, bringing an immense knowledge of languages and literature to bear upon the sources of Christian doctrine. But Christian humanism was not just an academic movement. The humanist's return to the sources echoes in a scholarly way the reformer's call to return to the simplicity of the primitive Church, and it represents a genuine piety, as one can see from reading the writings of Erasmus. Erasmus espoused a view of the Christian life boiled down to its basics: Do good, avoid evil, strive for humility. His *Enchiridion* or "handbook" for the laity focused on knowledge and prayer as the two "weapons" the Christian could use to defend herself against vice. The humanists combined tremendous eloquence and learning with simplicity of vision to form yet another vital reforming influence in the fifteenth and sixteenth centuries.

Numerous religious orders and institutions were either founded or re-founded in these years. The Oratory of Divine Love was a lay confraternity founded in 1497 in Genoa, Italy, and devoted to the corporal and spiritual works of mercy under the inspiration of St. Catherine of Genoa. This lay organization in turn produced a clerical order, the Theatines, who shared the Oratory's charism for service. In 1516, a passionate young Venetian layman, Gasparo Contarini, wrote a treatise *On the Office of the Bishop*, describing how a bishop, as a successor to the apostles, should act. The twist is interesting: While normal models of reform relied upon the clergy to reform the laity, here we see the roles reversed. It is the layman who is calling the bishops to account. Reform was in the air in the early years of the sixteenth century, even before Martin Luther's breakthrough, carried on in various ways by laity and clergy alike.

These many and various reform movements shared several qualities, what we might call *the platform of Catholic reform* in the sixteenth century. All of these movements shared a concern for the laity. Either they were lay movements themselves or they were clerical reforms that took a renewed interest in priests' missions and responsibilities toward the *laity*. Under the influence of the humanists, most of these reform movements promoted *literacy and education* as elements of their reform. For the first time, bishops and leaders of religious orders began to require that their clergy or postulants be literate, since only those who could read could be properly trained in their pastoral duties. Again under humanist influence, Catholic reform emphasized the importance of *Scripture* and of effective, persuasive *preaching* as essential elements in their program. Finally, many shared the conviction that devotion to the Eucharist was central to the work of reforming the Church, perhaps reflecting that the reform of the Body of Christ in head and members required a more intimate connection with the Body of Christ in the Eucharist. The members of the Oratory of Divine Love, for example, were required to "see the Body of the Lord every day" (*Oratory*, Chapter X, as quoted in Olin, *Catholic Reformation*, p. 23). All these elements combined to form a powerful Catholic reform program that was persistently presented to Rome in the early sixteenth century. But the effect upon the Roman curia, unfortunately, was slight. Something more significant would be needed to get their attention.

LUTHER'S BREAKTHROUGH

Martin Luther was born in 1483 and became an Augustinian canon in 1505. He was a very devout and zealous young monk, obsessed with his own sin. "In the monastery," he said later, "I did not think about women, money, or possessions; instead, my heart trembled and fidgeted about whether God would bestow his grace on me." Despite his personal scruples, Luther was a very effective monk, and after ten years in the monastery he was elected district vicar, in charge of ten monasteries. As vicar, Luther was a zealous reformer of the religious observance of his monasteries and an outspoken critic of the sale of indulgences. In an interesting way, this makes Luther very much a part of the Catholic reform movement in the years before his open conflict with Rome. The famous Ninety-five Theses, which he nailed to the church door at Wittenberg in 1517, were a trenchant critique of the indulgence practices. As such, they did not necessarily distinguish him from many of the other "troublesome" voices throughout the Church protesting the abuses of the Church. However, they did attract attention to him, and under the scrutiny he would receive from the authorities, a deeper and more unresolvable difference emerged.

The point of division between Luther and the Church was fundamentally a theological difference more than a dispute over particular Church practices. Luther had spent his life in search of God's mercy, and his rigorous practice of penance and asceticism in his early years as a monk reflected his attempt to discover that mercy and grace through the traditional medieval channels. But

Luther's sense of human sinfulness was so deep that he could not take comfort in medieval penitential spirituality. For him, it was impossible to imagine a human being ever becoming righteous enough to stand before God's judgment. To be righteous would mean to follow the Gospel perfectly, and he found this too difficult for any human to accomplish.

When he was teaching the letters of St. Paul at Wittenberg, however, he began to understand the "righteousness of God" in a different light. Rather than referring to God's just judgment, the "righteousness of God" began to seem to Luther to be God's free gift. It's not the active experience of working toward righteousness through penance; rather, it's the passive experience of receiving certainty of God's salvation through the gift of faith.

If this is true, it overturns the entire principle of medieval spirituality. If part of the human condition is to worry whether one is saved or not, the medieval answer had been to assure human beings of their own God-given strength: It's difficult, but you can do it with God's help. You can resist sin. For Luther, this is simply self-deception. The fact of the matter is that none of us is strong enough to always resist sin. Luther's answer is just the opposite: Luther assures you of your own *inability* to earn your salvation. You cannot resist sin, but salvation is God's work, not yours. And fundamentally, God is more reliable than you are in the matter of your own salvation. So for Luther, this is a doctrine of comfort. With all the responsibility for salvation upon God, one is not asked to accomplish the impossible. One cannot help but remain a sinner (for this is one's nature), but one can still be saved.

Since this doctrine entails a reversal of previous Catholic teaching on the relationship between grace and works and human nature, the natural question that Catholic theologians asked Luther was "How do you know?" On the one hand, how did Luther know that his doctrine, and not the doctrine of the Fathers and the Doctors of the Church, was correct? Furthermore, if Luther's concern is for the self-deceived sinner, how does he know that this doctrine and the comfort it brings are not themselves deceptions of the devil?

Both questions boil down to the issue of authority. For Luther, the authority of his teaching came from the "testimony of the Holy Spirit" within him as he read the Scriptures, bringing him comfort. Thus, the Spirit-filled individual had the authority to resist and overthrow the authority of the institutional Church. For Catholics like John Eck, with whom Luther disputed in 1519 at Leipzig, Germany, the opposition between the Spirit-filled individual and the Church was impossible. Christ had bequeathed the Spirit to the Church, and the Spirit preserved the Church from error. To suppose that the Spirit abandoned the Church of Peter to speak to one German monk was absurd.

Although Luther's fundamental insight was theological—a speculation on the nature of justification—and scriptural—based on his reading of the letters of Paul—his Catholic opponents pressed him to consider the implications of his insight on the nature of authority, and it is on this difference that the final break with Catholicism occurred. Under the scrutiny of Eck, Luther was forced to concede that he considered the authority of Scripture superior to the teaching of the Church and that his only resource for his interpretation of Scripture was the "testimony of the Spirit" as he read it. Eck's question in the Leipzig disputation, "Are you alone wise?" is said to have haunted Luther for the rest of his life.

Eck ended the Leipzig disputation with a plea to Luther to abandon his stubbornness and return to the Church. But Luther was convinced, and in conscience he could not retreat. In 1520, Rome issued a bull declaring forty-one of Luther's Ninety-five Theses to be heretical. Luther responded by publicly burning the bull. Alienated from the Church, Luther turned to the German political authorities around him for support. In 1520, he wrote three influential essays, *On the Nobility of the German Princes*, *On the Babylonian Captivity of the Church*, and *On the Freedom of a Christian*.

These essays were printed as pamphlets and distributed widely throughout Germany. In the first two, Luther played a political card. As we have seen, hostility between the German nobility and Rome was nothing new. In the first pamphlet, Luther praised the virtues of the nobility and validated their authority. In the second, Luther claimed that the Roman Church was captive, not of the French monarchy, as we have seen earlier, but of false teaching and heresy. The third treatise is a summary document of Luther's theology, in short, readable form. Luther, in essence, used these three documents to rouse the dissatisfaction of the German princes and give their "ritual complaints" a theoretical justification. When his official excommunication came in 1521, Luther appeared before the emperor of the Germans and issued his famous declaration, "Here I stand, I can do no other," and he retreated into the safety of a powerful noble's castle. The break with Rome was official.

Luther's break from Rome was like a spark that set off brush fires of rebellion against Rome throughout Germany and even in other parts of Europe. The speed with which Luther's ideas spread was due in part to the new technology of the sixteenth century: the use of the movable-type printing press in the early years of the century made the distribution of Lutheran ideas simple. Luther was a good publicist, too. He wrote thirty works between 1517 and 1520, and these probably sold more than 300,000 copies total. He often sent the initial chapters of works to press while he was still working on the last few, to be sure that the works came out immediately. By 1521, the German papal delegate, Aleander, was lamenting that "printers will not sell anything other than Lutheran writings." Luther's solitary stand on a matter of faith very quickly became a grand public affair.

But the support Luther gained was not simply due to the publicity, nor simply to the theological appeal of his teaching. Both of these were important, but it is questionable that these two factors alone were enough to accomplish the Reformation. Luther's rebellion against Rome had its political advantages. The nobility who protected him from the reach of the emperor and the pope saw the immediate political benefit to breaking from Rome. Supporting Luther meant freeing one's principality from the obligations of Church taxes and the meddling of Church authorities. In the towns, the councils had already assumed many of the social service responsibilities that the Church had usually provided; to some, it seemed quite natural to assume the religious responsibilities, too. In supporting Luther, the towns gained the power to appoint their own Church leaders.

Peasants, too, saw in Luther's declaration *On the Freedom of a Christian* a message of liberation from the constraints of the social structures that tied them to the nobility and the land. "Therefore do we find in Scripture that we are free," claimed a document published by the peasants of Swabia, "and we will be free." Luther had some sympathies with their demands for fair treatment, but he eschewed their violence and felt finally that they had misunderstood his message. As tales of the atrocities performed by peasants in his name came out, however, Luther wrote a tract exhorting the nobility to defeat the rebels by whatever means necessary. With this tract, Luther alienated much of the peasant support for his movement, but he strengthened his ties to the conservative townspeople and nobility.

By the time of Luther's death in 1546, nearly half of Germany's principalities and most of the free towns had sided with him and become "Lutheran." In those early years of the movement, the German emperor, sworn defender of Roman Catholicism, had been distracted by international affairs, fighting both France in the west and Turkey in the east, which left the lower nobility to make their own way. Only in 1547 did the emperor find the opportunity to attempt to regain his rebel provinces for Catholicism, and by that time it was too late. The skirmishes that continued for the next eight years made no decisive gains for either the Lutheran or the Catholic side. In 1555, the emperor reluctantly conceded to sign a truce, the Peace of Augsburg, which bound Catholic and Protestant alike to a non-aggression pact summed up in the *maxim cuius regio, eius religio* ("whosesoever region, his religion"). The religion chosen by the local noble would determine the religion of all in the region. The Peace of Augsburg was the first official recognition that Luther's protest had divided western Europe. The pope was no longer pastor to all Christians in western Europe.

The Varieties of Reform

It would be a mistake to characterize western Europe as simply split in two, Catholic versus Protestant. Luther was really just the first leader in the broad-based reformations that followed, and not all of these reformers agreed with one another. Quick on the heels of Luther's break from Rome, Huldrych Zwingli led a reformation movement in Switzerland that cast that land into open civil war and established what is generally called the Reformed Church tradition (ancestor to the Presbyterian and Dutch Reformed traditions today). Soon thereafter, the Reformed movement found its most systematic theological mind in John Calvin. These three—Luther, Zwingli, and Calvin—are generally considered the leaders of what is called the Magisterial Reformation, since their reforms focused upon particular points of doctrine or teaching (*magister* is Latin for "teacher"). While these three representatives of the Reformation agreed on the pervasive power of sin in human life and the sheer graciousness of salvation, they and their followers could not come to agreement in their sacramental theology or their theology of the Church. The debates that Luther had waged with his Catholic critics on the nature of authority came back to haunt the Reformation movement as the competing claims to the clear sense of Scripture and the inspiration of the Spirit plunged the movement into discord and in-fighting.

More threatening still to the order and harmony of the reform movement were the so-called Radical Reformers, the Anabaptists and Spiritualists, many of whom called into question the more fundamental tenets of the Christian faith. While Catholics, Lutherans, and Reformed churches could share a faith in the authority of the Holy Scriptures (the debate was more about who had authority to interpret them), Anabaptists relied more upon the "inner Word" of God within the soul. For an Anabaptist, Scripture had value as an outer testimony to this inner Word. Many Anabaptists taught that all humans would be saved, since God is perfect love. Anabaptists also emphasized the power of the human will to choose salvation, to make a decision for Christ, in sharp contrast to Luther or Calvin's perspective on the depths of human sinfulness.

Spiritualists went even further than Anabaptists. They rejected the Christian doctrine of the Trinity and any notion that the true, invisible Church of Christ had any relation whatsoever to the visible institutions of Catholicism or Protestantism. Anabaptists are the ancestors of the Mennonite and Amish communities, and Unitarian-Universalism has its roots in the Spiritualist reform. These dissidents were taken by Catholics and Protestants alike as threats to faith and good order, and both Catholics and Protestants were complicit in their persecution.

The last sphere of the Reformation movement, the English Reformation, was very different from any of the other movements, at least in its origins. While Luther, Zwingli, Calvin, and even the radical Anabaptists and Spiritualists undertook to reform (or abolish, as the Spiritualists might suggest) theology, the English Reformation was initially a dispute over the powers of church and state. Henry VIII, king of England, had written a scathing critique of Luther and the Reformation movement that impressed the pope so much that the king was honored with the title *Defensor Fidei*, "Defender of the Faith." When Henry's personal circumstances led him to declare himself head of the Church of England in the Act of Supremacy in 1534, the dispute looked more like a revisiting of the dispute between Pope Boniface VIII and the king of France in the early 1300s than an echo of Luther.

Nevertheless, the Channel did not isolate the English people from the influence of Protestant reforms on the continent, and in the following years reformers like Thomas Cranmer and Thomas Cromwell built a church that shared more with the Reformed churches than with the Catholics. The English Reformation is, of course, the beginnings of the Anglican Communion of churches, or what is usually called the Episcopalian Church in the United States.

By 1557, in the span of forty years since Luther's Ninety-five Theses, the face of Europe and the history of the Western Church had been changed forever. The kingdom of France was embroiled in bloody civil war, with Catholics pitted against Protestants. The German territories were split in half. The Scandinavian countries were firmly Lutheran; Spain was firmly Catholic. England forged its own brand of Protestantism, but Ireland remained stubbornly Catholic. The medieval ideal of Christendom, of a worldwide society united in a common faith, was dead. And the Catholic Church, for the first time since the Arian crisis a thousand years before, found itself face to face with a hostile rival for the souls of Europe. The lines of battle were drawn; the Catholic Counter Reformation had begun.

THE COUNCIL OF TRENT: ONGOING REFORM AND COUNTER REFORMATION

I have taken great pains to argue above that the movement for reform within the Catholic Church predates Luther's breakthrough and had a spirit of its own. The reform platform of the early sixteenth century—education, clerical reform, emphasis upon Scripture and preaching, devotion to the Eucharist—remained the issues at the forefront of Catholic renewal even as the Lutheran crisis broke out and spread. When Cardinal Alessandro Farnese became Pope Paul III (1534–1549), he immediately assembled in Rome a "dream team" of Catholic reformers, the best and brightest lights Catholicism could offer. Contarini, the fiery Venetian layman, was given the red hat of a cardinal in 1535. With him in Rome were Carafa, the founder of the Theatine Order (offshoot of the Oratory of Divine Love); Reginald Pole, an English humanist and exiled cardinal of England; Bishop Giberti of Verona, whose strict "reform constitutions" had revolutionized (and terrorized) his local clergy; and other such leaders. Together, they composed in 1537 the *Consilium de emendanda ecclesia* ("Recommendation on Healing the Church"), a report that laid bare with amazing candor the abuses and "wounds" of the Church and recommended "remedies" to heal them. The "wounds" were not at all surprising: clerical abuses, lack of education, poor and heretical preaching, and so on. What is significant is that the document was composed under papal authority; it represents a frank acknowledgment in Rome of the need for "healing."

While Pope Paul III's reasons for gathering Contarini and the rest surely had something to do with the threat posed by Luther's rapid success, the *Consilium* cannot really be considered part of the Catholic "Counter Reformation," the deliberate, intentional response to Protestantism. In fact, the Catholic reformers remained open to the possibility of reconciliation with the Lutherans, and Contarini himself led a Catholic delegation to the Colloquy (Conference) of Regensburg (in German, Ratisbon in French) in 1541. The Lutheran delegation was led by Luther's closest disciples, Martin Bucer and Philip Melancthon. Through a series of conversations and exchanges, Contarini and Eck (Luther's old adversary) and Bucer and Melancthon were able to come to a compromise agreement on the fundamental theological issues. The brightest theologians of both sides had agreed, and reconciliation, if not imminent, at least seemed possible. However, when the conference participants returned to their respective leaders, the agreement collapsed. Both Luther and the pope rejected Regensburg as compromising too much, and so the conference of Regensburg, called in the hopes of unity, in the end served only to clarify the depths of the disagreement. The last hopes of reconciliation were dashed.

It is from this point on that I think we can talk about a Catholic Counter Reformation. After Regensburg in 1541, Catholic reformers' efforts shifted from searching for common ground to clarifying differences. Contarini, the soul of Catholic reform, took ill within a year, bringing a close to this first chapter in the Catholicism of the sixteenth century in a tragic but somehow fitting way. A new era of Catholic reform began, an era that combined Contarini's reform platform with an aggressive anti-Lutheran/anti-Protestant *ethos*. Almost prophetically, the Society of Jesus, the enthusiastic order of priests and brothers who would lead this new wave of reform, was founded and chartered in 1540. But the culmination of the new reform came in the Council of Trent.

The Council of Trent (1545–1563) represents Catholicism's systematic response to the Protestant Reformation. The Council was a moment of self-definition for the Catholic Church, and we still live with its legacy. Its decrees are both the natural extension of Contarini's reform platform and the calculated response to the ideas of Luther and Calvin. Trent first took up one of the basic bones of contention between Protestants and Catholics: the authority of Scripture. The Council declared that the Vulgate, the Latin translation of the Bible that St. Jerome and his contemporaries had made, was the authoritative version of Scripture, free from dogmatic error. The decree provides a definitive list of the books in the Catholic canon and affirms that the fullness of revelation is found *both* in the written books of Scripture *and* in the unwritten traditions. The wording of this decree was carefully chosen to refute the Protestant equation of revelation with Scripture without diminishing Scripture's significance. Trent declared that the Catholic Church, as the custodian of both the written and the unwritten elements, was the only sure and reliable authority in the interpretation of Scripture.

Trent also issued a decree on justification and grace, the point of fundamental theological difference that Regensburg had failed to overcome. Against Luther, Calvin, and Zwingli, Trent declared that original sin does not undermine our ability to cooperate with God's grace. While Luther taught that original sin was so debilitating that human beings could not help but sin, Trent taught that the effects of original sin left us with an inclination toward sin, but that this inclination could be resisted. According to Trent, it is an essential truth of the Catholic faith that human beings must cooperate with God's grace in salvation.

The decree on the sacraments integrates the Catholic reformers' emphasis upon the centrality of the Eucharist with an anti-Protestant polemic. Luther and Calvin had searched for the biblical foundations of the traditional sacraments and found them wanting. They affirmed only Baptism and the Lord's Supper, and they had disagreed even upon the nature of the latter of these. Trent affirms that there are seven sacraments and confirms the doctrine of transubstantiation in the Eucharist. According to Trent, the substance of the Body, Blood, Soul, and Divinity of Christ are really present in the Eucharist under the *accidents*, the appearance, of bread and wine (see *CCC*, #1413).

Thus far, most of the decrees seem to reflect the anti-Lutheran dimension of the Catholic Counter Reformation. But the last decree—and one of the longest— picks up the fundamental issues that Contarini's reformers had expressed in *the Consilium de emendanda ecclesia*; namely, the rights and responsibilities of the bishop. The Council fathers called all bishops to take responsibility for the enforcement of their reforms. Their decrees strengthen the authority of the local bishop over his church, giving him authority to speak "in the name of the pope" and to establish seminaries for the education and training of his clergy. After three long sessions that stretched out over eighteen years, the Council of Trent was finally closed on December 3, 1563. From a Catholic point of view, the Reformation crisis had ended. Catholic doctrine had been reaffirmed against Protestantism, the structures of authority had been strengthened, and, perhaps most significantly, Catholicism had emerged with a firm sense of confidence, identity, and mission.

❧✝❧

For Reflection

1. Where are the seeds of reform in the contemporary Church? How can we learn from the mistakes of the past and prevent Christianity from further divisions?

2. In the contemporary Church, we may hear the phrase *Ecclesia semper reformanda*, the Church is always in the process of reforming. If this is true, if we are always reforming, what elements of the "Catholic reform platform" are still in need of implementation today? What new elements would you include?

3. What have you heard about the Council of Trent before? Did reading about the context and the history confirm or challenge your image of the Church at the time of the Reformation?

CHAPTER 5

Faith in a New World

With the close of the Council of Trent, the Catholic Church emerged from the shock of the Reformation and began to face a new world with renewed passion. The mantle of spiritual leadership was taken on by new or newly reformed religious orders. Among them are many of the orders that still minister in the Church today: the Ursulines, the reformed Discalced (or "barefoot") Carmelites of Teresa of Avila and John of the Cross, the Sisters of the Visitation founded by Francis de Sales and Jeanne de Chantal, and the Capuchin Franciscans all took an active role in the Tridentine (meaning "related to Trent") renewal of Catholicism. Missionaries from the Dominicans, the Franciscans, and many others spread throughout the newly discovered territories of the world. All of this vitality and movement can be traced through Trent to the late-medieval "platform" of Catholic reform. But the renewal of religious life in the Counter Reformation after Trent is perhaps best exemplified in the Society of Jesus (the Jesuits). This new order, founded by St. Ignatius Loyola and his companions, grew at an incredible rate of speed in the mid- to late-sixteenth century and spread throughout Europe and beyond. In many ways, the Jesuits can serve as the "test case," a representative example, of the spirit of the Catholic renewal that followed Trent.

St. Ignatius and the Jesuit "Way of Proceeding"

St. Ignatius of Loyola was born in 1491 in Guipúzcoa, a Basque territory in northern Spain. He was born into a noble family. His youth and young manhood were devoted to the courtly life of chivalry and romance. His success in courtly pursuits seemed to promise a good career in politics or diplomacy. But when French troops invaded and threatened to take the city of Pamplona, Ignatius and his countrymen joined the defense force. The commander of the Pamplona garrison realized that the French possessed superior forces and planned a retreat, but Ignatius and his fellow Basque countrymen refused to leave—a move that was both courageous and stupid, as Ignatius later admitted freely. When the French artillery breached the garrison walls, a cannonball passed right between Ignatius's legs, shattering one and severely burning the other. When Pamplona fell, he was treated by the French surgeons and returned to his castle in Loyola to recuperate. Unfortunately, the bone was not set properly and had to be rebroken and reset. When it had healed for the second time, it was a bit misshapen, so the vain young courtier asked for further surgery to shave the bone down, doubling his recovery time. (In the end, the shaving procedure wasn't quite successful; Ignatius spent the rest of his life slightly disfigured and walking with a limp.)

During his long convalescence in the castle at Loyola, Ignatius was hungry for reading material. The only books he could find were a collection of the lives of the saints and a meditation on the life of Christ. These two texts had a profound effect on Ignatius, so that, once he had recovered from his injuries, he no longer wanted to be part of the courtly world and decided instead to embark on a pilgrimage to Jerusalem. The first leg of his journey brought him to Manresa, a town in Spain. His intense prayer experiences at Manresa led him to develop certain principles of the spiritual life, which he brought together in a book he called the *Spiritual Exercises*. When weather and politics prevented him from continuing his journey to Jerusalem, Ignatius instead returned to school at the universities of Alcala, Salamanca, and Paris. In the midst of his studies, he began to guide several of his classmates through his *Spiritual Exercises*. These classmates became the founding members of the Society of Jesus.

The *Spiritual Exercises* are a series of guided meditations given over four weeks that assist one in "plumbing the depths" of one's own spiritual life. In some ways, it represents the typical late medieval piety we have already seen in the "Modern Devotion," with its interiority and its vivid portrayal of the life of Christ. But, unlike other late medieval spiritual writings, the *Exercises* does not make interiority an end in itself. Rather, the "discernment of spirits" he advises is always directed toward a moment of decision, a commitment, or an action, based upon the wisdom, confidence, and guidance gained in the course of the *Exercises*.

Ignatius aimed to set the soul in motion, to create "contemplatives in action," and he appended to his *Exercises* a set of "Rules for Thinking with the Church" to help direct this motion in a proper direction. His thirteenth rule requires obedience and faith even against reason and perception: "If we wish to be sure we are right in all things, we should always be ready to accept this principle: I will believe that the white that I see is black, if the hierarchical Church so defines it." This "activist" spirituality, strict in its obedience to the "hierarchical" (i.e., Catholic) Church and rigorous in its discipline, helped make the Jesuit order the standard-bearer of the Catholic Counter Reformation in the years after the Council of Trent.

The Bull of Institution that established the order with the papal stamp of approval in 1540 issues a call to "[w]hoever wishes to be a soldier of God under the banner of the Cross and to serve the Lord alone and His Vicar on earth in our Society." This military metaphor portrays vividly the action-oriented nature of Ignatius's new group, and he defines the order by the actions it will undertake: the society is "a community founded principally for the advancement of souls in Christian life and doctrine and for the propagation of the faith by the ministry of the word, by spiritual exercises, by works of charity, and expressly by the instruction in Christianity of children and the uneducated" (Olin, p. 83).

All the elements of the Catholic reform platform are found in this brief statement: the emphasis on preaching, on prayerful interiority, and explicit attention to education of the laity. In addition, the beginnings of the Counter Reformation are also here: strict obedience to the pope, the Vicar of Christ, is set forth from the very beginning, suggesting the "closing of the ranks" in Catholicism that we see in the 1540s. The first Jesuits vowed in this document that "whatever His Holiness commands pertaining to the advancement of souls and the propagation of the faith we must immediately carry out . . . whether he sends us to the Turks or to the New World or to the Lutherans or to others, be they infidel or faithful" (Olin, p. 84). Jerome Nadal, one of Ignatius's early companions, described the Jesuit lifestyle, what they called their "way of proceeding," in a nutshell: Jesuits proceeded "in the Spirit, from the heart, practically." This insightful blend of spirituality and practicality, of contemplation and action, allowed them to carry forward the banner of Tridentine Catholicism into the world.

THE MISSION TO ASIA

The Jesuits were, in fact, among the first called into the "New Worlds" (new at least to Europeans) of Asia and the Americas. After Columbus's famous journey in 1492, the European powers, especially Spain and Portugal, seemed to catch "expansion fever." At the request of the king of Portugal, St. Francis Xavier, one of Ignatius's original companions and a fellow Basque, departed for Asia in 1540, even as the order received formal approval from the pope. He arrived in Goa, India, in 1542 and established there a base camp for the Asian missions. In 1549, he journeyed to Japan, where he found what he thought was a noble civilization: "We shall never find among heathens another race equal to the Japanese. They are people of excellent morals—good in general and not malicious." The Jesuits encountered Zen Buddhist priests immediately upon their arrival in Japan. Quickly discerning the similarity of their roles, the Catholic missionaries immediately made cassocks out of the orange cloth that identified the Zen priests to the culture. In Asia, this process of adaptation and assimilation was essential to the success of the missions. After some time in Japan, Francis Xavier heard tales of the great civilization and culture of the Chinese across the sea. He had begun his journey there and reached the shores of the Chinese mainland when he died in 1552.

Though Xavier did not complete his journey into China, some of his brother Jesuits did soon after his death. When they found Buddhist priests among the Chinese, they immediately assumed their dress and manner, thinking that what worked in Japan would also work in China. However, China had a strict sense of class and privilege, and Buddhist priests were considered lower-class people. The people of influence in China, the *mandarins*, were Confucian.

Confucianism is a religion—perhaps better, a moral philosophy—based on the teachings and precepts of Confucius (Kung fu-tse), basically conservative in nature, emphasizing loyalty, family, and tradition. Jesuit missionaries like Matteo Ricci and Johann Adam Schell von Bell saw no inherent conflict between Confucianism and the Gospel, and therefore they grew out their hair and beards in the Chinese manner, wore mandarin clothing, and studied the teachings of Confucius even as they developed relationships with the Chinese nobility and began to teach about Christianity.

One might pause to wonder here why it is that the Jesuits were not content to work among the poor and lower classes like the Buddhist monks they had initially imitated. After all, Christ had worked with tax collectors and sinners; shouldn't missionaries do the same? Would, say, Franciscans, for whom poverty is so central an idea, have acted differently? Perhaps, or perhaps not. For better or for worse, it seems likely that the Jesuits, as good European Tridentine Catholics would, had a structured hierarchical image of society. When they came to China, they found a similar structure. In India, the caste system invested the societal hierarchy with religious value; one Jesuit, Roberto de Nobili, lived for thirty-seven years as a *sanyassi*, a holy man of the upper caste, wearing ochre robes, wearing no leather, eating no meat, learning Sanskrit (the Indian classical language), and refusing contact with other Europeans. For him, this was the appropriate way of making the Gospel make sense in this foreign culture. In a hierarchy, the most effective may to proceed with change is to start at the top and allow ideas to "trickle down" into lower classes. And indeed, Ricci, Schall von Bell, and de Nobili each had a considerable amount of success in their mission.

The fundamental question behind all these actions is fascinating, but difficult. How much can missionaries adapt and assimilate without violating the core of the Christian message? Where is the line between culture and faith? Were Matteo Ricci and Roberto de Nobili "going native," or were they struggling to understand the culture in order to express the Gospel in a meaningful way? These questions came to the fore in what has come to be called the "Chinese Rites controversy." The Jesuit mission's superior, Alessandro Valignano, had written directives for missionaries in 1579 that made Jesuit priorities clear:

> Do not attempt in any way to persuade these people to change their customs, their habits, and their behavior, as long as they are not evidently contrary to religion and morality. What could be more absurd, indeed, than to transport France, Italy, or some other European country to the Chinese? Do not bring them our countries but the faith, which does not reject or harm the customs and habits of any people, so long as they are not perverse; but, on the contrary, wishes to see them preserved in their entirety.
>
> (quoted in Hsia, p. 187)

Ricci was able to take these directives and put them into practice. His first publication after arriving in China was not a Chinese translation of a Christian catechism, but rather a Latin translation of the Confucian *Four Books*. He and his successors presented Christianity as a system of social ethics entirely consistent with Confucianism; in fact, Jesuits aligned with Confucian reformers in an effort to purge Confucianism from the "contamination" of Buddhist thought and used Christian moral principles to do this. Ricci's brilliance with the Chinese language and his willingness to learn from the mandarins and adapt attracted a few powerful converts in the Chinese court, converts who would be instrumental in defending and promoting Christianity in China. Did this inculturation go too far? Perhaps. The Jesuits in China did not speak much of original sin and other points of doctrine that were not so easily aligned with Confucianism. They also refrained from displaying crucifixes for fear of offending the civilized sensibilities of the Chinese. Suffice to say, the questions raised by inculturation are great and heavy.

Ricci's strategy received initial support from Rome; in 1621, Pope Paul V approved the celebration of Mass in Chinese and allowed certain Confucian rituals to be incorporated into the liturgy. But a few other Jesuits raised objections to these practices, as well as to the use of Confucian terms for "Heaven" (*Tian*) and "God on High" (*Shangde*) instead of transliterations of the Latin terms. These opinions were shared by the Dominican missionaries that had followed the Jesuits into China, and a great propaganda war on behalf of the Chinese missionaries began in Rome. In 1645, the Holy Office of the Inquisition condemned Confucian religious rites as heathen practices incompatible with true faith. The Jesuits appealed, and in 1656 Pope Alexander VII reversed the decision. The tide shifted for and against the Jesuits for the next fifty years, until Pope Clement XI's legate to China declared to Emperor Kangxi that Confucianism had been condemned. Kangxi reacted swiftly, declaring that all missionaries in China must follow "the way of Father Ricci" or be expelled from the empire. This rift between the emperor and the pontiff damaged the mission to China seriously. While Catholicism survived in China, it lost much of its audience and thus, perhaps, much of its influence upon the Chinese people.

The mission to Japan suffered a fate even more tragic. After some initial success in the region around Nagasaki, the Christian mission was soon drawn into Japanese feudal politics. Several powerful *daimyo*, or "warlords," had converted to Christianity. As these lords fell into and out of favor, so, too, did the Christian faith. When Ieyasu Tokugawa became *shogun* or "overlord" in 1599, Buddhism was promoted to unify the Japanese under him. In 1614, Tokugawa ordered all foreign missionaries to leave Japanese soil. When several stayed behind, hiding in villages and continuing their evangelical work, they were tortured or killed. The Japanese did not wish to create martyrs, so they developed brutal tortures to compel missionaries and Japanese Christians to apostatize or reject Christianity, as Japanese novelist Shusaku Endo portrays so vividly in his novel *Silence*.

In all, the Asian mission bloomed quickly and withered almost as fast. The great Catholic experiment of incultured missions had failed. To this day, Japan and China remain among the nations least touched by the Christian faith. But the other "New Worlds" of the sixteenth and seventeenth centuries were to be deeply affected by the missionary effort. In the Americas, missionaries pursued a different strategy, both more effective and perhaps more troubling in the long run.

THE MISSIONS TO THE AMERICAS

The missions to the Americas actually began before the Reformation. Franciscan and Dominican missionaries had followed the Spanish into Central and South America after Columbus. Unlike the Jesuits in Asia, the American missionaries came to the Americas as part of a conquering force. Christianity was therefore the religion of the culture imposed upon the conquered peoples. While the Spanish crown valued the missionary opportunity of the New World, they believed that possession of the land had to precede the evangelical goal. Cortés conquered the Aztecs in Mexico in 1521, and Pizarro took the Incan Empire in Peru in 1536. In both cases, missionaries followed quickly in their footsteps. But this is not to say that the missionaries were simple pawns of Spain and the entrepreneurial conquistadors. In fact, as early as 1511, when the conquering forces in the Caribbean began to exploit the native populations as a free labor source, a conscientious missionary named Antonio Montesinós preached a Christmas Day sermon on the text from Isaiah, "A voice cries out in the wilderness," in which he speaks of the indigenous peoples in the "West Indies":

> They are crying, I tell you. They are crying out from the pain of injustices visited upon them. They are crying out for the Good News which we preach, the Good News of salvation that comes in word and deed, not at the end of the master's whip.

Pleas such as this continued for many years. The most famous missionary-advocate is Bartolomé de las Casas. He was the first priest to receive ordination in the New World. De las Casas was a great pamphlet writer, and his numerous writings sometimes tweaked the conscience of the Spanish people and eventually won protection from slavery for the native people under Spanish authority.

One of the most successful forms of missionary work in the South American territories again came at the hands of ambitious Jesuits. The Jesuits were relative latecomers to South America, arriving only after 1570. One of their centers of influence was in the rain forests around the Rio de la Plata (present-day Paraguay, Uruguay, and Brazil), the home of the Guarani tribes. The missionaries set up settlement camps, reducciónes, for individual Guarani tribes. The sacraments were administered in the indigenous languages, and local Guarani music and dances were incorporated into the liturgical life right alongside traditional European rites. The native members of the reducciónes lived with their property in common, with their own leadership. In fact, they also organized their own armies, supplied with weapons by the Spanish viceroy in Lima, to defend their tribes against bands of slave traders. The missionaries served as chaplains, physicians, and negotiators with the colonial authorities, but they left the details of government and community life to the Guarani. For a time, it seemed to be an ideal model of the Christian mission.

However, after nearly 150 years of this sort of life, world politics intervened upon the peace of the Guarani. When Spain and Portugal renegotiated a territorial treaty in the 1750s, the Guarani in Uruguay were forced to evacuate their *reducciónes*. When they refused, their Jesuits joined them in an armed rebellion that was crushed by Spanish and Portugese troops. This tragic tale is beautifully portrayed in a successful 1987 film, *The Mission*, which shows how compelling this story can still be to the imagination. The story of Catholic missions in South and Central America is the story of politics, race, and religion crossing over, conflicting, resolving, and sometimes collapsing into chaos. As in Asia, the history is filled with moments both tragic and comic. The story of North America, unfortunately, would be no different.

The Catholic Church came to North America in several different waves. The southwestern territories were part of the Spanish conquest. The French settled eastern-central Canada, the Great Lakes region, and the Mississippi Valley, or what became known as the Louisiana Purchase. Finally, and perhaps least often considered, a number of English Catholics settled in Maryland (the only colony established by Catholics) in the seventeenth century as they sought a safe haven for their faith. The English Catholics came for peace, not mission; the mission work to native populations was undertaken mostly by the Spanish, whom we have already discussed, and the French, who worked in the Great Lakes region with the Iroquois and Huron tribes.

The French had first established contact with the Hurons and, since the Hurons and Iroquois were enemies, the latter proved to be quite resistant to the approach of the missionaries. With the Hurons, however, they had greater success. The French Jesuit settlement camp, Ste. Marie, in Ontario served as a sort of home base where missionaries could gather and regroup before they fanned out, either individually or in pairs across the St. Lawrence River valley. There they ministered to Huron villages—roughly 12,000 Hurons in all—and they reported nearly 1,000 baptisms between 1633 and 1635. However, the Iroquois constantly threatened and attacked the Hurons, putting many missionaries in harm's way. The martyrdom of several of these Jesuit missionaries, especially Jean de Brebeuf, Gabriel Lalemant, and Isaac Jogues, has become part of the tradition of the American Catholic Church, celebrating the courage and tenacity of these men of faith.

The World at War: Europe in the Seventeenth Century

With the exciting developments abroad in the New World, it could be easy to lose track of what was taking place in Europe, the homeland out of which all these Jesuits, Franciscans, and Dominicans came to preach the Good News. Times in Europe were difficult; as Catholicism emerged from the Council of Trent with renewed life and vigor, so, too, was it willing to face Protestantism as a serious opponent. Lutherans and Calvinists were no longer regarded as errant children, but as sworn enemies. Lutheranism and Calvinism, too, gained strength in the middle and late years of the sixteenth century. Skirmishes and conflicts became as inevitable as a fight between two bullies. In Luther's time, the first wave of conflicts in Germany had ended in a truce, *cuius regio, eius religio* ("whosesoever domain, his religion"). But unfortunately, the Peace of Augsburg in 1555 was the beginning, rather than the end, of the bloody conflict between Protestants and Catholics that continued for a century.

Almost as soon as Augsburg had settled the German conflicts, wars of religion broke out throughout France. Open warfare between French Calvinists, called *Huguenots*, and Catholics began in 1562 and continued on and off for forty years and more. Much of the conflict came over the royal succession, with Catherine de Medici, acting as the head of the Catholic League and as regent for her son, the child king Charles IX, and Henry of Navarre, cousin to the king, leading the Huguenots. Henry himself inherited the throne in 1598. He converted to Catholicism in order to become King Henry IV, but he quickly acted to protect the interests of his former Huguenot compatriots. He issued the Edict of Nantes in that same year, guaranteeing Huguenots toleration and freedom of self-government in the southern and western territories of France. Very conservative Catholics—called *ultramontanes* because they looked "beyond (*ultra*) the mountains (*montane*)" for leadership from Rome—did not trust Henry's conversion to Catholicism, and Henry was assassinated in 1610 by a Catholic student. Even with the declaration of toleration, the bitter struggle between Protestant and Catholic continued.

In the German territories, the political juggling between Protestant and Catholic princes continued. Although there was little open combat, each side constantly sought to outmaneuver the other politically, hoping to shift the balance of power decisively one way or the other. In 1618, the king of Bohemia, one of the designated electors of the German emperor, shifted his kingdom from the Catholic to the Protestant side. Fear that this would be the last straw that tipped the scales decisively toward the Protestant cause, Catholics took up arms. The tension between Protestants and Catholics throughout Europe was so strong that this local German conflict sparked a massive brush fire of religious war that swept across Europe.

The Thirty Years' War, as the conflict came to be known, was perhaps the first "world war" in European history. While most of the warfare (and thus most of the devastation) took place in the German territories, the conflict drew all the "superpowers" of the seventeenth century into the fray, with wealthy Spain coming to the aide of the Catholic side as a new player in the European theater, and Lutheran Sweden wading into European affairs on behalf of the Protestants. Though the war did in fact continue for thirty years, it ended in a stalemate. The Peace of Westphalia in 1648 established the German toleration principle, *cuius regio, eius religio*, as the rule of law throughout Europe, despite the objections of Pope Innocent X that certain clauses of the treaty were offensive to Catholic faith. The princes of Europe, Protestant and Catholic alike, weary from the years of war, preferred peace and toleration to defiance or obedience. Stability was more important than truth. The peace held.

From Momentum to Inertia: The Catholic Church on the Eve of Revolution

The two centuries after the Council of Trent saw the renewal of Catholicism's confidence in its own mission and identity. On the European continent, Catholicism faced Protestantism as an adversary to be fought and would underestimate it no more. At the same time, the colonization of the New World provided the Church with a new outlet for its evangelism. Bruised and beaten a bit, faced with the strife and violence of the wars of religion at home, the Church turned to the mission field as a fresh beginning and a new horizon. At the edge of this new horizon stood many religious societies committed to the missions—the Franciscans, the Dominicans, and the Jesuits, to name a few.

We have taken a more detailed look at the Jesuits in this era, not to suggest that they stood alone in this work (they did not), but because the Society of Jesus, in its very constitution and unique spirituality, embodies the spirit of the Tridentine Church in a particularly clear and distinct way. It is perhaps fitting, then, that we should end the story of this era with the (first) end of the Jesuit order. By the mid-eighteenth century, the Society of Jesus represented a vast network of power and influence, spread throughout the known world. In a world subdivided into spheres of political influence wielded by absolute monarchs, the Jesuits alone seemed to transcend the boundaries and extend their clandestine influence across borders.

Power, of course, raises suspicions, and if Lord Acton's observation is correct, that power corrupts, then perhaps such suspicions were merited. Whatever the merits may have been, these suspicions rose to a fever pitch in 1759, when the royal court of Portugal had the entire Jesuit order expelled from its realm. France followed suit in 1764, and finally, Spain, too, rejected her native son's Society in 1767. The ban was made binding throughout the Catholic Church by a formal decree of abolition by Pope Clement XIV in 1773. All Jesuit operations—schools, missions, parishes, local and abroad—were to be closed or turned over to the local bishop. Only the "enlightened despots" of eastern Europe—Frederick II of Prussia and Catherine the Great of Russia—dared to defy the papal ban, more out of scorn for the pope than sincere interest in the Jesuits' survival. The vanguard of Tridentine Catholicism was abandoned, cut off from the Catholic powers of Europe and thus from the New World, left to limp along in the far-eastern corner of Europe.

This is perhaps a fitting place to end this chapter. While the Society of Jesus eventually was exonerated and restored early in the nineteenth century, the momentum of the Counter Reformation which they had carried for two centuries to the ends of the earth was lost. Jesuit-trained leaders of the Enlightenment like Voltaire would be among the first to fire the volleys that would put the Catholic Church back on the defensive. The restored Jesuits, who had once led the charge, were often left to defend the ramparts of the Church as revolution swept around the world in the eighteenth and nineteenth centuries.

❦✝❦

FOR REFLECTION

1. How do you balance action and contemplation? What would it take for you to be a "contemplative in action" like the Jesuits?

2. With Matteo Ricci in mind, how can you express the faith to others who do not share your culture?

CHAPTER 6

Faith in an Age of Revolutions

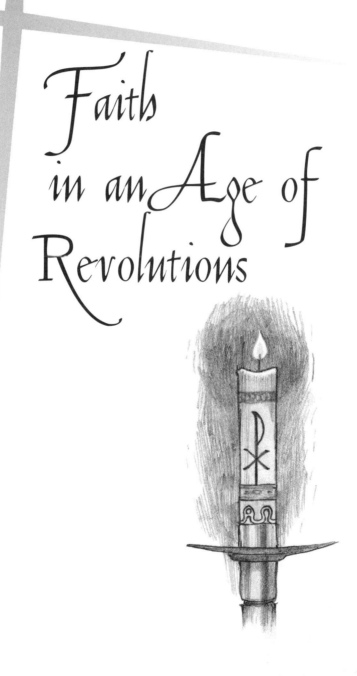

W hile the Church stood on the vanguard of the New World in the missions, it was by no means a force that stood entirely for progress. In the face of certain revolutions, both intellectual and political, from the seventeenth century into the twentieth, the Catholic Church, rightly or wrongly, has often resisted the forces of change that confront it.

The Church and the Scientific Revolution

Perhaps the first of these great modern revolutions that the Tridentine Catholic Church faced was the Scientific Revolution. The notorious conflict between Galileo Galilei and the Catholic authorities in the early 1600s is well known. But the roots of this conflict reach back deeper into the era of the Reformation, in the person of Nicholas Copernicus (1473–1543).

Copernicus was a faithful Catholic living in the Polish countryside. Astronomy was for him a religious exercise, a spiritual discipline, a way of listening to the harmony of God's creation. His years of work led him to refine the theory of the structure of the universe. For reasons both scientific and theological, Christian scientists had supported Aristotle's ancient understanding of a *geocentric* universe—a universe in which Earth is at the center and the planets and stars revolve around it. Copernicus was able to demonstrate mathematically that the evidence made at least as much sense if the Sun, not Earth, lay at the center. This *heliocentric* ("sun-centered") theory was controversial, as Copernicus knew well. He withheld the publication of his book until the end of his life and, as the story goes, he received the first copy from the press upon his deathbed. When his work was finally published, Protestants and Catholics alike condemned it as heretical.

Galileo Galilei (1564–1642) was not the first to suffer trial and condemnation for supporting and defending the Copernican thesis, but he was certainly the most famous. The central issue, of course, was whether Copernicus's theory was correct. Galileo believed that he had demonstrated its truth experimentally through the use of the telescope. His initial findings were published in a work entitled *Starry Messenger* in 1610. This work and those that followed set off a debate over Copernicus's theory, but even more, about the role of the Bible in scientific investigation, about the relationship between theological and scientific truth, and about whether truth is always observable (i.e., whether an important phenomenon like Earth's revolution could possibly be true when we cannot feel or see it moving).

It was a difficult and thorny issue, and while we now know that Galileo's model is more accurate than the geocentric view, such proof was not available to the disputants on either side, and the defenders of geocentrism could give an account of the evidence one could observe with the naked eye. While, as the Catholic Church has recently discussed, the trial of Galileo involved some mistakes among the parties representing the Church, the Church officials were not simply stupid or authoritarian or wicked. Instead, it seems, they were caught on the frontier of a new world of the mind, the world of science, the landscape of which was marked by technological and theoretical innovations like the telescope and the experimental method. After disputes on and off over the next twenty-five years, Galileo's theories were condemned in 1633 and he was placed under arrest in his own home, where he stayed for the remainder of his life. He died in 1642.

Shots Heard 'Round the World: Revolution in America and France

The early modern period was also a time of the great political revolutions, with the Americans leading the way. On the face of it, the American Revolution doesn't seem to have much effect on the history of the Catholic Church—at least not immediately.

The British Empire was not Catholic by any means, and the colonial insurrection of Washington, Franklin, Adams, Jefferson, and the rest might seem to be simply a matter of internal imperial politics. While a few of the signatories of the Declaration of Independence were Catholic (e.g., Charles Carroll of Maryland), their Catholicism hardly seemed to enter into their politics.

But the American Revolution is a watershed moment in the political and intellectual history of Western civilization. The Revolution represents the political "first fruits" of the intellectual movement that had the self-confidence to call itself the Age of Enlightenment. These concrete political actions taken on the authority of Enlightenment principles set the era of revolutions into motion, so that even when Enlightenment thinkers like Jefferson had passed, the revolutionary ideal survived and spread.

The self-proclaimed "Enlightenment" was an intellectual movement that began in the early years of the eighteenth century and reached its apex in the 1770s and 1780s. Immanuel Kant, one of the movement's most influential philosophers, defined *Enlightenment* as "man's emergence from his self-imposed immaturity." For Kant, institutions such as the Christian churches substitute tradition and dogma for reason and investigation and thus permit individual human persons to remain immature and to neglect to think for themselves. Kant finds it impossible to believe that any creed or doctrine passed on in a tradition can be invested with authority by rational people, since this would keep them from progressing in their understanding. The Enlightenment confronted the authority of tradition with what it took to be the superior opposing authority of reason. Traditional religions, political institutions like monarchy, the legal authority of local custom, all should be dissected by the critical edge of a person's own reason. The Catholic Church, one of the most tradition-centered institutions in history, naturally became a target for these thinkers on the European continent.

The American Revolution, then, represented the first attempt to bring together Enlightenment ideas to wrest authority away from a traditional monarchy and establish a new government on rational principles. The principles of the American experiment were not founded upon a royal authority divinely bestowed or on precedent established by five hundred years of trial and error, but rather upon assertions about inalienable human rights, democracy, separation of church and state, and rationally balanced powers of governing. While the American founders did draw on classical exemplars and early modern political theories, the sum total was novel and perhaps a bit unsettling to common assumptions about the nature of tradition and authority.

Thus, while the American Revolution itself had little direct effect on Catholicism, it set the revolutionary spirit in motion. The French Revolution of 1789 followed close on the heels of American independence and declared a new government founded upon principles similar to those of the American founding. French political thought before the Revolution had made no attempt to separate religion from politics or, more especially, Catholicism from politics. King Louis XIV had revoked the Edict of Nantes that his predecessor had issued to protect the Protestants, so only Catholics had the rights to be considered true subjects of the crown. The most influential advisors to the Bourbon kings were men of the cloth like Cardinals Richelieu and Mazarin, and the Estates-General, the French advisory body to the king, was divided into three separate houses (something like our House and Senate) of clergy, nobility, and commoner. The Catholic Church was thus very much a part of the *ancien regime*, the old order of society and government against which the Revolution acted.

The early actions of the revolutionaries in relation to the Church seemed mild and, for the most part, were directed toward correcting some of the "ritual complaint" abuses in the ecclesiastical bureaucracy. But the storming of the Bastille on July 14, 1789, was the beginning of a more radical phase of change. In 1790, the National Assembly—the revolutionary government—had formed a commission directed by a bishop to reform the Church hierarchy. The result was the Civil Constitution of the Clergy, which essentially made the Church a department of the national government. The pope was relieved of his jurisdiction over the French Church, although the constitution still contended that the French Church would remain in communion with him. Thus, the government felt no need to consult with Rome before it required French clergy to swear an oath of loyalty to the Civil Constitution. Many, of course, did so and formed what became known as the Constitutional Church, but many did not and chose to remain *ultramontane*, loyal to the pope alone. The French Church was in schism over this issue for ten years.

Unfortunately, this was but the tip of the iceberg of the Church's woe. The Revolution progressed and grew more and more radical, culminating in the "Reign of Terror." The leaders of the Terror waged an active campaign to eliminate Christianity or any such "superstitions" and replace them with a cult of the goddess Reason or a rational religion that honored the Supreme Being. The great Notre Dame Cathedral in Paris was converted into a Temple of Reason. Both the Constitutional and the ultramontane churches found themselves under attack; yet both, somehow, survived. In France, the "eldest daughter of the Church," as it has been called, Catholicism seemed too deeply rooted to be extirpated by radical ideology. But, even so, both churches were forced to minister to the French people in secret, since the anti-Catholic, anti-religious spirit of the Revolution remained in force among the governing elite.

The Church was able to emerge from the shadows only when Napoleon Bonaparte seized power and bestowed stability and order on a society turned upside-down by a decade of revolution. Napoleon knew that religion can serve to unify a people, and therefore he negotiated with Rome to reunite the Constitutional and ultramontane churches under terms he more or less dictated. Napoleon became head of the French Church, and all the Church property confiscated by the state in the Revolution remained in his hands, but the Church was once again in communion with Rome, and the pope reluctantly agreed. The Catholic Church had survived the Revolution, but the face of French Catholicism had changed forever.

LIBERALS AND ULTRAMONTANES:
FRENCH CATHOLICISM AS A TEST CASE

The effect of the French Revolution was not isolated to France; in varying ways, the revolutionary spirit spread throughout the European continent, and even to some degree into England. Historian Norman Cantor counts it among the four great "world revolutions" in Western history because of its lasting effect on the European mind. To cover all the countries and areas where this influence touched upon Catholicism would take far more space than I can allot for this chapter, so, as in the last chapter I chose the Jesuits as the best example of the Counter Reformation of the seventeenth and eighteenth centuries, so here I will focus first upon France, and then upon America as the two places most acutely affected by the revolutions of the late eighteenth century.

The Napoleonic settlement left the French Church in a strange position. It was at once conservative (in support of Napoleon's new empire) and revolutionary (insofar as it was legally separated from Roman authority). As it tried to stay afloat through the tempest of several more revolutions or changes of power, French Catholicism struggled to come to terms with both its faith and its new relationship to the political order. It was in response to the ambiguity of this murky limbo that both liberal Catholicism and a renewed ultramontanism emerged.

Paradoxically, both responses can trace their roots to one person, Félicité de Lamennais (1782–1854). In the early part of his public life, Lamennais was associated with a group of reactionary Catholics led by a writer named Joseph de Maistre. De Maistre attributed all the ills of society to the French Revolution, where the focus on individual rights had given every person license to do whatever he or she wished, with no respect for a moral order. The only relief for this revolutionary infection could come from a return to authority—in matters of politics, to strong legitimate monarchs, and in matters of religion to the Church of Rome. Initially, Lamennais supported this integration of royalism and ultramontanism.

However, he soon decided that the monarchy was not a reliable source of authority, and he cast his lot with the revolutionary ideal of liberty. As historian Alec Vidler has suggested, his strategy shifted from trying to exorcise the Revolution to trying to baptize it. For Lamennais, this was entirely consistent: if the monarchy was a liability to true faith and not an ally, why not cut Catholicism free from it and allow the faith to thrive on its own in a state in which religious liberty was protected? But Lamennais and his movement were rejected by the bishops, and when they appealed to Rome, they found Pope Gregory XVI, feeling threatened himself by revolutionary activity in his own papal states, unwilling to listen to their case. In the encyclical *Mirari vos* in 1832, the pope condemned the liberal Catholic movement without any doubt.

That Lamennais was part of both the liberal and the ultramontane movements may seem strange, but in the postrevolutionary world of France in the 1830s and 1840s, there was a certain logic to the connection. The Revolution had severed ties between the state and the Catholic Church. For liberals, this was an opportunity: with the state fully secularized, the Church could be free to flourish in a world in which its liberties were protected. On the other hand, the secularization of the government pressed ultramontanes to look more and more to Rome for spiritual and juridical authority. Both parties agreed on the separation of the Church from the current regime. This uneasy alliance of liberal and ultramontane survived until 1848, when revolution again struck France, and this time it spread throughout continental Europe.

Pius IX: Reform and Reaction

The revolutions of 1848 proved to be a decisive turning point for Catholicism in the nineteenth century. In the 1830s and 1840s, as the Church sputtered to life again in the wake of the French Revolution, it appeared after a few fits and starts that a moderate liberalism would prevail in its ranks. Indeed, Giovanni Mastai-Ferretti, a known sympathizer with the liberal nationalists in Italy, was elected pope in 1846, taking the name Pius IX, or "Pio Nono," as he was affectionately called. Conservative Robert Wilberforce complained of the "pretty state we are in" in early 1848, "with a Radical Pope teaching all Europe rebellion." Italian nationalists even floated the idea of uniting Italy into a democratic federation under Pio Nono. Catholic liberalism seemed to be the reigning philosophy.

However, all this changed in the spring of 1848 when revolution broke out across the continent. In Italy, the nationalists struggled against the Austrian army in the effort to gain independence and unify Italy into a nation. As pope, however, Pio Nono could not afford to choose sides between a reigning Catholic sovereign and the Italian revolutionaries. Almost overnight, the pope's popularity collapsed. Throughout the papal states, and even in the city of Rome itself, public outcry and hostility toward him was so great that Pius fled Rome in fear for his life. When the Austrian troops finally suppressed the nationalists, Pius returned to Rome a changed man. Burned by the anger of the liberal nationalists, Pio Nono turned his back upon liberalism of any sort; the rest of his long pontificate was devoted to the centralization of ecclesiastical authority and the promulgation of dogmas—among them, the Immaculate Conception of Mary in 1854 and papal infallibility in 1870.

Pio Nono's reactionary turn is perhaps best represented in his *encyclical Quanta cura* in 1864, which condemned liberalism, socialism, communism, and secularism. These four, said Pius, represented all the social evils of the age. The encylical itself condemned the movements in the most general fashion, but to the document was attached a *Syllabus of Errors* that specified particular concepts and practices that constituted the four general philosophies. Among the principles condemned were the separation of church and state, freedom of the press, and freedom of religion. All of these condemnations were summed up in the last statement in the *Syllabus*, which denied that "the Roman pontiff can and ought to reconcile himself and reach agreement with progress, liberalism, and modern civilization." Pius did not sign the *Syllabus*, so it does not fit within the category of definitive teaching. But his message was clear enough.

Soon after the publication of the *Syllabus*, Pius announced his intention to convene a general council. Liberal Catholics were initially pleased and even relieved, since they believed that the injustices and mistakes in the pope's recent declarations could be challenged and corrected. However, it soon became clear that this was not to be the council's agenda. Just before the First Vatican Council convened, a document emerged from Rome that suggested that the sole purpose of the Council would be to declare the dogma of papal infallibility. Liberal Catholics were in the minority; they were able to debate the point and moderate the language used to define what infallibility was, but they could not defeat it. Nearly sixty bishops left the Vatican and returned home before the final vote. When the vote was cast, 553 bishops supported the declaration; only two voted no.

Pio Nono held the See of Peter longer than any of his predecessors, for a total of thirty-two years. Though despised by educated liberal Catholics throughout Europe, he never failed to keep the support of the "common believers." He was a charismatic person whose presence, according to John Henry Newman, was "magical." He combined a simple affability with genuine piety and warm humor; he granted numerous audiences to all sorts of visitors in Rome. This warmth and generosity seems difficult to square with his ardent conservatism of condemnation. Perhaps even Pio Nono himself knew this. At the end of his pontificate, very near his death, he commented:

> I hope my successor will be as much attached to the Church as I have been and will have as keen a desire to do good; beyond that, I can see that everything has changed; my system and my policies have had their day, but I am too old to change my course. That will be the task of my successor.

America and Americanism

Among those who left the Council rather than vote for infallibility were several prominent American bishops, above all Archbishop Peter Kenrick of St. Louis. Kenrick was a scholar as well as a bishop, and while in Rome he composed two pamphlets that questioned the arguments for infallibility by invoking the traditional teaching of the Church. Catholicism had taken on its own character in the United States, where it lived and worked of necessity within just the sort of constitutional system that Pius IX condemned. This experience gave American Catholicism a particular sense of identity and, eventually, led some American Catholics to the brink of excommunication.

In the early years of the United States, Catholicism was the religion of a more-or-less silent minority of citizens, and it really didn't factor into public policy much at all. However, as European immigrants arrived on America's shores, they brought with them their Catholic faith and heritage. Between 1790 and 1860, the number of Catholics in America grew from thirty-five thousand to over three million. From about 1820 on, Catholicism had a very public presence in the major cities of the United States as the religion of the working-class immigrants. Unfortunately, its presence was not always welcome. In the 1830s, a run of anti-Catholic pamphlets and books poured off presses all over America. The burgeoning Catholic populations responded in kind; many of the major diocesan newspapers were founded in this period as an effort to return fire in the propaganda war. For anti-Catholic "nativists," Catholics were traitors to America by the very fact of their allegiance to the pope, a "foreign power." Many spoke of a clandestine plot, sponsored and led by the pope, to invade and conquer the Mississippi Valley. Tensions were high, and violent conflict was inevitable.

In the 1840s, rioting broke out in many of the major industrial cities that the Catholic working class inhabited. Rioting in Philadelphia in the summer of 1844 killed many Protestants and Catholics, and much of the city was set on fire. In Louisville, Kentucky, August 6, 1855, became known as Bloody Monday after Catholics and nativists had clashed and left twenty-five dead and hundreds wounded. As rumors of nativist activity reached north to New York, Archbishop John Hughes demanded a meeting with the mayor and threatened that if one Catholic church was burned, the whole city would be set afire. "We can protect our own," he said, "I come to warn you for your own good." Hughes's inflammatory challenge may not be the best example of "turning the other cheek," but it was effective. A nativist rally at City Hall was cancelled, and violence was averted.

Anti-Catholicism eventually spawned its own political campaign. The Native American Party was formed in 1843 with the intent of excluding Catholics from any public office and taking other such measures to limit the influence of the "foreign power" upon American life. The party was affiliated with a secret society called the Order of the Star-Spangled Banner, whose favorite slogan was George Washington's directive, "Put only Americans on guard tonight." The party's practice of secrecy eventually gave them the nickname of the "Know-Nothing" Party. The Know-Nothings actually mounted a presidential campaign in 1856, with ex-president Millard Fillmore at the head of their ticket. The political life of the Know-Nothings ended with the Civil War, but their legacy is still felt in that other secret society, the Ku Klux Klan.

This experience of hostility and persecution led American Catholics to become, if anything, "super-patriotic," trying to prove that Catholics could be excellent citizens. Many Catholics fought and died in the Civil War. As early as the 1830s, Alexis de Toqueville, the astute observer of American life, could conclude that "Catholics in the United States are at the same time the most submissive believers and the most independent citizens." The leaders of the American Catholic Church in the late nineteenth century grew up with this double identity. Of necessity, many Catholics were forced to be the sort of liberals that Pius IX condemned in France. But the Americans initially attracted little attention, at least until the century's end and the so-called Americanism controversy.

The controversy was sparked by one of America's most creative Catholic thinkers. Isaac Hecker (1819–1888) was born and raised in a family influenced by the American Transcendentalist movement, a very individual-oriented mysticism best represented by Ralph Waldo Emerson. In 1844, Hecker converted to Catholicism and soon became a priest in the Redemptorist order. However, Hecker envisioned a new order of priests whose spirituality and ministry would be particularly attuned to the needs and sensibilities of contemporary Americans. He founded the Congregation of Missionary Priests of St. Paul the Apostle, or the Paulists, with this in mind. Hecker's Catholicism was orthodox and he supported the decision of Vatican I on the infallibility of the pope, but he balanced this understanding of authority with a deep trust in the activity and guidance of the Holy Spirit in each individual person in the work of spreading the Gospel. He also affirmed the value of democracy and religious freedom in the American context.

Hecker's activist spirituality, individualism, and positive approach toward democracy and religious liberty were echoed in the prominent leaders of American Catholicism in the late nineteenth century. Archbishop John Ireland of St. Paul, Minnesota; Bishop John J. Keane, rector of the Catholic University of America; Monsignor Denis O'Connell, rector of the American College seminary in Rome; and James Cardinal Gibbons of Baltimore all sought useful ways of accommodating Catholicism to fit American culture and to Americanize the Catholic immigrant population. Many of their actions struck conservatives as overly conciliatory toward the American system, and several were censured or pressed to resign their positions. The first major notice Rome seemed to pay to American Catholicism was not particularly praiseworthy.

Things came to a head after Hecker died in 1888 and, in 1897, his biography was published in France. The French introduction to the biography praised Hecker as the model priest for the future: more active than contemplative, more at home in the streets than in the cloister. The French edition of this text found its way to

Rome and, together with several documents collected from O'Connell and Keane, became the evidence for a curial investigation into what was dubbed "Americanism." In 1899, Pope Leo XIII, Pio Nono's successor, issued *Testem benevolentiae*, an apostolic letter condemning "Americanism," which to him seemed to mean the "watering down" of doctrine until it was palatable to modern people. Gibbons and Ireland quickly denied that any such heresy had ever been taught or promoted, but the archbishops of New York and Milwaukee thanked the pope for thwarting the heresy they had seen on their doorsteps. The "Americanism" controversy divided the American bishops and made those former crusaders for reform more timid and reserved in their actions.

The Early Twentieth Century: Catholic Modernism and the Stirrings of Change

The Catholic Church at the turn of the twentieth century dwelt in the shadow of Pius IX and the First Vatican Council, with a strong notion of papal authority, a passionate and even sentimental piety, and a deep suspicion of innovation. Leo XIII's famous and influential 1891 encyclical *Rerum novarum* shows a real development in Catholic social teaching in support of labor and unions, but Leo himself was still very much a pope in the model of Pio Nono. However, the late nineteenth century had seen the flourishing of Catholic centers of learning in Tübingen, Germany, the Institut Catholique in Paris, and the Catholic University in America, among others. The scholars of these institutions struggled to come to terms with the developments in philosophy and historical criticism in a Catholic fashion. The debate came to center on technical questions of philosophy. In his 1871 encyclical, *Aeterni patris*, Leo XIII had declared that the "Christian philosophy" of Thomas Aquinas (or "Thomism") is the best model for Catholic thinkers to follow. But modernist scholars looked beyond Thomas Aquinas to philosophers of the modern period as they reflected on the nature of revelation and tradition.

According to *Pascendi gregis*, Pope Pius X's 1907 letter of condemnation, "modernism" was a diverse movement that shared two principles that were incompatible with the Catholic faith. Firstly, he said, modernists denied metaphysical reason, the notion that rational thought could understand something of the reality outside of time and history. Secondly, modernists denied the supernatural and thought of revelation as an interpretation of what happens within the realm of nature. Whether the particular individuals who were accused of modernism actually subscribed to these beliefs is an unsettled question. But the message was clear: Catholics were to be cautious in their use or appropriation of other philosophical thought. However, the modernist crisis was, in effect, only the first episode in the conflict between tradition and innovation as Catholic philosophers and theologians continued to explore the edges of Thomism.

Perhaps in part because they had been discouraged from exploring the new, certain theologians in the 1930s and 1940s sought to reinvigorate theology by a return to the old. Young French scholars like Henri de Lubac and Jean Danielou began to take a fresh look at patristic and early medieval thinkers, at St. Augustine and St. Ambrose and St. Gregory the Great, to find a theology that had a sense for the aesthetic and the pastoral and was closer to Scripture than the neo-Scholastic theology of their teachers. This "return to the sources" became the hallmark of what was called the New Theology and it was sharply resisted by more-traditional Thomists. Nevertheless, despite all opposition, the New Theology set the tone for much of the work that would emerge from the Second Vatican Council. De Lubac and Danielou were both appointed as cardinals before their deaths.

American Catholicism at Mid-Century

In America, the Catholic population continued to grow throughout the first half of the twentieth century. With the coming of the First World War, Catholics readily enlisted in greater proportion than any other minority, and fought side by side with Protestants. Catholic soldiers returned home to receive much more respect as citizens than they had previously enjoyed, and now felt fully a part of American society.

As the rest of America plunged into the "feel-good" era of the Roaring Twenties and beyond, Catholic culture remained strangely aloof. Historian William Halsey has suggested that Catholics in the years between the wars enjoyed a strong sense of self-confidence and a real distance from the disillusionment that marked much of American and European culture after World War I. The beginnings of what we can call a "Catholic ghetto culture" were beginning to take shape, a culture in which Catholicism echoed the culture around them and yet attempted to remain at a distance. Sharing in the postwar prosperity, Catholic bishops began great construction enterprises, and new churches sprung up quickly in the major urban and industrial centers. In the Catholic ghetto, thinkers read Catholic novelists, discussed Catholic politics, and so on. The creation of this culture was facilitated by the opening of Sheed & Ward Publishing House in 1933. Frank Sheed and Maisie Ward, both accomplished authors in their own right, undertook to publish books by great European Catholic authors like G. K. Chesterton, Jacques Maritain, and Paul Claudel. Sheed and Ward aimed to provide Catholics with the intellectual material to create an American Catholic humanistic culture.

The Catholic leadership in the early part of the century complemented this cultural revival with ongoing work toward social reform. The bishops continued to serve as advocates for the laboring classes and sought to develop Catholic social teaching on economics in order to fit the very particular needs of the American worker. The initiative to work with the needs of the poor came from the laity as well. In 1933, Dorothy Day began distributing her *Catholic Worker* newspaper for a penny a copy, advocating the cause—and attempting to meet the needs—of the urban poor. At about the same time, Baroness Catherine de Hueck, an aristocratic immigrant from Russia, established the first Friendship House in Harlem. Within the next decade, she opened more Friendship Houses in major cities. These houses tended to the needs of the urban poor, offering them opportunities, and acting as public policy advocates on their behalf.

Catholicism at mid-century was thriving in America. It was at its height, with strong leadership, ample resources, stimulating intellectual life, and a vibrant social justice community. The Second Vatican Council could only complete and extend the reinvigoration that had already begun in the Church.

$$\mathbf{\mathcal{K}}\!+\!\mathbf{\mathcal{K}}$$

FOR REFLECTION

1. Catholics in America in the nineteenth and twentieth centuries constantly struggled to harmonize their Catholicism with their American identity. Are there times when we feel tension between our identity as Catholics and our identity as Americans?

2. Reform or revolution often happens, not when things are at their worst, but when things are beginning to get better. What do you think about the pre-Vatican II Church? Has this brief summary of the history supported or challenged what you thought before?

CHAPTER 7

Conclusion: Faith Handed On to the Third Millennium

On October 11, 1962, Pope John XXIII opened the Second Vatican Council. Soon after his election as pope, in early 1959, John had expressed his intention to call a council. This cherubic pope, supposedly elected as a "safe" pontiff since, at his age, he could not accomplish much, had with this action already done just that. The Second Vatican Council, like the Council of Trent that had adjourned three hundred years before, was a moment of formation and re-formation for the Catholic Church. But unlike many previous councils, the gathering John envisioned was not to combat a particular heresy or face a particular crisis, but rather to contribute to the work toward the unity of humankind so that "the earthly city may be brought to the resemblance of that heavenly city where truth reigns [and] charity is law." He criticized the "prophets of doom" around him who "can see nothing but prevarication and ruin" in the modern world. John envisioned an *aggiorniamento*, an "updating" of the Church so that it could open its arms to the modern world as "the loving mother of all, benign, patient, full of mercy and goodness toward the brethren who are separated from her." If the Council of Trent had been about the strengthening of identity through the clarification of difference, John's council was to bring this process full circle, to bring about a renewed openness to the world.

Of course, as we have seen in the last chapter, it would be a mistake to think that the Church to whom John was speaking was closed off from the world, inactive, or stagnant. John's predecessor, Pius XII, had been an activist pope himself. During the Second World War, Pius XII had challenged and denounced fascist and Nazi policies toward the Jews and had sponsored rescue missions for Italian Jews through Catholic religious houses and institutions. In recent years, critics have accused Pius of failing to condemn Nazism explicitly. However, closer study of his public proclamations and their reception in Europe make such accusations ring somewhat hollow. On the contrary, Pius was perceived during the war as a crusader against the Axis powers.

In addition to his political activism, Pius had sponsored or supported many of the scholarly and cultural initiatives we saw discussed in chapter 5. His *Divino afflante spiritu* (1943) had ratified Catholic biblical scholars' moderate use of modern historical-critical methods; *Mediator Dei* (1947) had given papal support and inspiration to the movement for liturgical reform that had just begun. His encyclical on the Church, *Mystici corporis* (1943), had cautiously opened the possibility for ecumenical dialogue. Many of the initiatives that we usually associate with the Second Vatican Council had begun and been approved by the pope in the years before the Council gathered.

So what made the Council itself different? The first factor is John himself. While Pius XII had been a shrewd and diligent leader, he struck one as aloof, magisterial, and stiff. John, on the other hand, had an affable simplicity that was attractive to all who met him. His charismatic presence seemed to emanate the sort of openness to which he was summoning the Church. Then there was the very fact of the Council's assembly. Vatican II was the largest and most ecumenical assembly in the Church's history. (Vatican I had been the largest to that date, with 773 bishops in attendance, most of whom had been born and raised in Europe.) Nearly three thousand bishops contributed to Vatican II, and more than half of these came from outside Europe and North America. While many of the influential voices in the Council were still European, this critical mass that more and more represented the universal Church changed the atmosphere of the Council.

In the first session, several bishops moved to reject the preparatory documents and to draft new ones. The papal curia had seen to the preparation of the draft documents for the Council fathers to consider, and while these had introduced some innovative ideas for reform, they generally followed the cautious, tentative manner that Pius XII had displayed in his encyclicals. But the influential voices among the assembled bishops were interested in more than tentative proposals. When the drafts were discarded, the contours of the Council, and thus of the Catholic Church in the twentieth century, changed.

The Council convened in four sessions; Pope John XXIII saw only the first. Even before the Council convened, he was diagnosed with stomach cancer and knew he would not live to see the end of it. When he died in June of 1963, Council business was interrupted for a papal conclave, and Cardinal Montini of Milan, one of the stronger reforming voices, was elected on the third ballot of the first day and took the name Paul VI. The remaining four sessions of the Council moved rather quickly, perhaps from the vigor that momentous change often brings. The last session was adjourned and the Council was closed on December 8, 1965.

Vatican II produced sixteen documents on a variety of doctrinal and pastoral issues. Among the most important and often cited today are the *Dogmatic Constitution of the Church (Lumen gentium)* and *the Pastoral Constitution on the Church in the Modern World (Gaudium et spes)*. *Lumen gentium* is the most systematic treatment of the theology of the Church ever to emerge from a council. It declares that the Church is "in the nature of a sacrament—a sign and instrument, that is, of communion with God and of unity among all men." (#1) *Lumen gentium* thus speaks of the Church as a means, not an end. It speaks of the Church as constituted both by bishops and clergy and by the laity, each in their respective places of witness in society. The document calls all in the Church to a life of holiness and hope for the coming of the Kingdom of God.

The *Pastoral Constitution on the Church, Gaudium et spes*, is the longest document produced by the Council. It emerged in the last sessions as a form of direct address to the whole world. While *Lumen gentium* could be seen as an internal document, *Gaudium et spes* might represent a proclamation and an invitation to the world. Rather than starting with a reflection upon Scripture and tradition, it begins with an empirical discussion of the human condition in the modern world, and then it moves to reflect upon this condition in light of the Gospel, a mode of argument that would be imitated by liberation theologians and by the U.S. bishops in their pastoral letters. It is one of the few documents to emerge from any council that remains readable and compelling to an audience broader than "church specialists."

The issues handled by the other documents were very specific, and some of the changes we most often associate with Vatican II are rooted in these. *The Constitution on the Sacred Liturgy (Sacrosanctum concilium)* recommended vernacular liturgies and encouraged priests to ensure that liturgies gave ample opportunity for the "full and active participation by all the people" (#14). *Dignitatis humanae*, the *Declaration on Religious Freedom*, for the first time recognized the fact of religious pluralism without condemning it or lamenting it. Instead, the document argued that religious freedom is a principle rooted in the freedom of conscience: any decision for faith or against it must be made by a conscience free from any compulsion or restraint by secular or religious authority. In effect, this declaration reverses the trend in Catholic thinking on liberal democracy, making a moment of reconciliation between Catholicism and classical liberalism again possible.

Vatican II changed the landscape of the Catholic Church. For younger Catholics, who have only known the postconciliar Church, the older Tridentine liturgy seems as strange as the rites of another religion. For some older Catholics, the deep sense of disillusionment they felt when they arrived one Sunday in church to find the altar turned around and the priest speaking in their local language may still linger on. But opinions on the legacy of the Church are not simply divided along generations. The Church of the late twentieth and early twenty-first centuries must still struggle to come to grips with the meaning and momentum of the Second Vatican Council.

For some conservatives, the Council itself was a mistake. Several Catholic prelates rejected its authority from the very beginning and even broke with Rome. The movement led by Archbishop Marcel Lefebvre denied the legitimacy of the Council because, they claimed, it reversed Catholic teaching on modernism and had thus broken with the apostolic tradition. Lefebvre was suspended from his priestly duties and eventually excommunicated in 1988 for ordaining bishops without papal authority. After this break, the movement split between those who sought to remain in communion with Rome and those who rejected it. The former formed the Priestly Fraternity of St. Peter, a conservative order of priests with papal permission to be trained and to minister in the Tridentine Latin liturgy. The latter are gathered around two groups, the Society of St. Pius X and the Society of St. Pius V, forming their own "faithful remnant" Church out of communion with Rome.

Of course, most reactions to the Council were not quite so dramatic. Most Catholics are willing and even eager to accept Vatican II, but it still remains to be seen what the proper form of this acceptance should be. An intellectual battle is being waged over the proper sense and significance of the Second Vatican Council. Neither the "liberals" nor the "conservatives" show any signs of flagging strength, or flagging will either. In Charles Morris's recent book *American Catholic*, he offers a case study of two diocesan communities in the contemporary U.S.—Saginaw, Michigan, and Lincoln, Nebraska. Saginaw is led by Kenneth Untener, one of the more liberal of the American bishops. Lincoln's bishop is Fabian Bruskewitz, perhaps the most outspoken representative of the more conservative bishops. What is fascinating about the study is how vibrant and alive both communities seem to be—though each community seems to tend toward a particular sort of piety, both seem deeply committed to the Church and its mission. Both communities seem to attract young and old. One wonders if the case study reveals an American hunger to "stand for something," and that it matters less what that "something" is. But whether one end of the spectrum will have the last word on what that "something" is for Catholicism in the next millennium is difficult to say.

In a broader world context, the same polar trends can be seen. The liberal cause has drawn much of its inspiration and intellectual nourishment from the liberation theologians of Latin America. For the most famous of these, Gustavo Gutierrez, liberation theology is a theology that begins from the experience of the poor and oppressed. It is a movement that emphasizes the continuity between justice and dignity here and now for God's people and salvation for all eternity, and thus calls for an integration of the "mystical" and the "political." Some liberation theologians have been criticized in Rome for oversimplifying the relationship between political justice and eternal salvation, and it seems fair enough to say that the political dimension lies at the forefront of their concerns. Liberation theologians often emerge from "base communities," small, local, grassroots gatherings of families of poor farmers and workers committed to prayer, justice, and mutual support. The success of these communities has led to the development of the "base community" ideal in other non-Latin American contexts and an emphasis for some Catholics upon social justice as the cornerstone of Catholic identity. Catholic theologians who share these concerns often write for a journal founded in the wake of the Council called, fittingly enough, Concilium (Latin for "council"). The editors of the journal perceive that they are about the business of continuing and extending the work of Vatican II.

On the other side, there are Catholics who are concerned that the "spirit of Vatican II" has been taken well beyond the parameters originally intended by the Council fathers. To these, it seems that the Church's concern to be open to the modern world and primary emphasis upon social justice run the very serious risk of watering down the truth and cutting away the richness and particularity of the Catholic tradition. They believe that liberation theology and other post-Vatican movements sacrifice the mystical for the sake of the political or, even worse, fuse the two without distinction. Several lay and clerical movements that seem to share these concerns have grown and spread around the world, among them *Opus Dei* from Spain and "Communion and Liberation" from Italy. Henri de Lubac, S.J.—one of the founders of the "New Theology" movement and a theological expert at Vatican II—was of this opinion for the last fifteen years or so of his life. So, too, was Hans Urs von Balthasar, the idiosyncratic Swiss theologian. Joseph Cardinal Ratzinger is perhaps the most articulate spokesman for this concern in the Church today. Writers in favor of this position often appear in one of a series of federated international journals called *Communio*. (Again, this is fitting enough, since they seek to preserve the mutuality of communion with God and community with others.)

But what does all this mean? Both "liberals" and "conservatives" in the Catholic Church today claim that their actions are natural extensions of the Second Vatican Council. Could it be that both are right? We have seen throughout this book that the story of faith handed on is sometimes filled with conflict and bitter dispute. We have also (hopefully) seen that even this conflict can be productive of insights essential to the development of the Church. Whether it be the clarification of the doctrines of the Trinity and Christology in the ancient Church or the conflicts between popes and emperors over the nature of Church authority in the medieval Church, or even the divisive struggle over the Protestant Reformation movement, we have seen some good come out of these things. It is my conviction that the struggle of the next century will be over precisely this matter in coming to terms with the Second Vatican Council.

As it stands now, "liberals" claim social justice as their proper preserve, as the fulfillment of the call of *the Pastoral Constitution of the Church in the Modern World*. "Conservatives," it seems, prefer to reflect upon *Lumen gentium*, the *Dogmatic Constitution of the Church*, to focus upon the essential nature and identity of the Church in relation to Christ. Are these two mutually exclusive? If they are not, we need to take great care in discerning how they are consistent. Conservatives claim to be the guardians of the piety of the Church—its oneness with Christ. Liberals prefer solidarity with the world. The question that should guide the Church of the twenty-first century is, "Can we find a way of life, a spirituality for a Church that is united with Christ and in solidarity with the poor?" Can we have a Church that is both *mystical* and *political*, with neither term sacrificed to the other? If so, how?

Ad fontes! Return to the sources of the Christian faith for inspiration and guidance! I suspect that the answer to such a question will not come from conversations, although I applaud initiatives like the late Cardinal Bernardin's "Common Ground" project for opening the lines of communication. I suspect rather that the solution, if and when we find it, will grow out of the charism of a saint, someone whose keen insight into both

Church and world can penetrate into the heart of the matter and find a way of living out the Gospel that is both mystical and political, ever ancient and ever new.

Many years ago, Saint Augustine was spurred on to his conversion by hearing the story of St. Anthony of Egypt. Centuries later, Hildebrand, who became Gregory VII, was inspired to view the entire world in a different light by the story of the early Church as portrayed in Acts and by the example of St. Benedict. St. Ignatius of Loyola was converted by reading about Saints Francis and Dominic. Such is the legacy of Church history at its best. We are constantly renewed and reborn when we return to our own sources. It is my hope and my prayer that we in the Church will find inspiration to end the battle that seems to take place every day.

Church history is the story of faith handed on. In this brief book, I have tried to hand on to you in some short form what I myself have received: that Christ died for our sins in accordance with the Scriptures, that he was buried, and that he was raised on the third day in accordance with the Scriptures; that Paul's witness to this truth was passed on to the early Church; that thousands upon thousands of faithful souls, popes and laymen and women, for nearly two thousand years, have struggled to live out the Gospel of this Crucified and Risen One; that they have succeeded sometimes, and that sometimes they have failed; and that their lives, their struggles, and their faith can sharpen our eyes and open our hearts to face the challenges of the Gospel here and now; finally, that, with God's help, we will continue the tradition and hand faith on to the next millennium. Amen. Amen.

BIBLIOGRAPHY

Dawson, Christopher. *Religion and the Rise of Western Culture*. New York: Doubleday-Image, 1991.

    This one you could read cover to cover. It talks about the general trends of medieval culture and civilization and the role of religion in them. It's great for a snapshot view of the medieval world.

Evennett, H. Outram. *The Spirit of the Counter-Reformation*. Notre Dame: University of Notre Dame Press, 1970.

    Evennett studies how the Catholics reformed themselves through a mix of reformed piety, new apostolic vision, and new governmental structures. More an interpretive essay than a historical narrative—so it is essential that one have some background on the figures and events he discusses. Particularly good on Ignatius and the Jesuits.

Frend, W. H. C. *The Rise of Christianity*. Philadelphia: Fortress Press, 1984.

    This is an enormous book, but it is invaluable as a resource for learning more about the first five hundred years or so of the history of the Church. I wouldn't recommend reading it from cover to cover, but it's good to pick up for a chapter here and there.

Hsia, R. Po-Chia. *The World of Catholic Renewal: 1540-1770*. Cambridge: Cambridge University Press, 1998.

    A wonderful book that introduces the Catholic Reformation with a comprehensive view. A good chapter on the Chinese Rites controversy.

McBrien, Richard, ed. *The HarperCollins Encylopedia of Catholicism*. New York: HarperCollins, 1995.

    This is an excellent general reference for things historical and contemporary. If it has a bias, it's probably more to the left than to the right, perhaps reflecting the personality of its editor. But, on the whole, it's readable and reliable.

Morris, Charles. *American Catholic*. New York: Random House, 1997.
    Morris is a journalist, not a historian, so he's very readable. But
he takes the time to get his information pretty straight. A good
start for the history of the American Catholic Church.

Olin, John C. *Catholic Reform: From Ximenes to Trent*. New York:
    Fordham University Press, 1992.
    This very helpful short book identifies milestones of Catholic
reform prior to, during, and after the Reformation. It has a brief
interpretive essay and a collection of important historical sources
in translation.

Vidler, Alec. *The Church in an Age of Revolution, 1789–Present*.
    London: Penguin Press, 1971.
    This is just a great introduction to Church history in the mod-
ern period. Its scope is broader, since it includes all of Western
Christianity. Well-written, too.

Acknowledgments

About the Author

Kevin L. Hughes, Ph.D., is an Arthur J. Ennis Postdoctoral Fellow at Villanova University. He has taught courses on a variety of themes in Church history, from early Church history to liturgy to the Protestant and Catholic Reformations. He has been a catechist and adult education speaker on history and spirituality for parishes in Chicago and Philadelphia. His doctoral degree is from the University of Chicago Divinity School in the history of Christianity. His particular interest lies in medieval Church history.